Time Bomb Tommy

Autobiography by
Tommy Crockett

ISBN 978-0-9855660-5-0

Published by The Elim Group 2023

Printed in the United States of America

Table of Contents

Introduction

This masterpiece is written by a guy who got a solid D in two semesters of Communication my Freshman year at Pitt State.

I remember my Dad telling the story that when he and Mom would write letters to one another, Mom would send page after page. He would sit and scratch his head trying to think of something to say, so he had his sister Betty help him write.

In that regard, I took after my Dad. So here goes....

Chapter 1
Early Years

Walter Lee & Marjorie June Bunton Crockett

I was born June 16th, 1941, in Lamar, Missouri. My folks were Walter Lee and Marjorie June Bunton Crockett. My first years were spent living in Irwin, MO where my Dad owned the grocery store.

Grocery Store in Irwin, MO

Tommy Joe & Walter Crockett

Without God's help, I wouldn't have been here. First, when I was nine months old, I became very sick. Mom took me to Dr. Bickle who said that I was just constipated. She was to go home and give me a laxative. There God had His hand on me because if she had given me the laxative, it would have killed me.

My Grandad Barney told Mom & Dad to take me to another doctor. They took me to Dr. Duckett. After looking at me, he told my folks to get me to Kansas City as fast as they could. My intestines had become kinked.

After my operation, I was a happy guy and they couldn't keep me down. Dr. Duckett told my Aunt Inez that I had lived two days longer than I should have.

My first ticking time bomb. More about that later because I will have more of them.

WWII was going on. Dad sold the store to his sister, Inez and moved over to Verdella, MO to farm with my Grandpa Emmet Bunton. We lived in a house that Grandpa owned, the place where our daughter, Michelle and her husband, Doug now live.

Tommy Joe Crockett, Jessie & Emmet Bunton

In the Fall of 1944, my sister, Louise was born on November 14. I couldn't go in the hospital but Mom held her up by the window so I could see her for the first time. One day, I remember Mom putting her in a buggy and we walked down to Grandma Bunton's. It was a long way to push a buggy on a gravel road; it was almost two miles from where Michelle lives now to where Chad, Michelle's son, lives on Grandpa and Grandma's farm.

One memory I have of that house was on a Halloween, we heard a ratty-tat-tat on our windows. Dad snuck out the back door and came back with three kicking and squalling boys. Turned out to be Jim, Tom & John Noyes. Dad lined them up in front of us for apologies. I asked John a couple of years ago if he remembered it. Yes, they had taken nails, wound them in rubber bands, went up to the window and let them spin. He said they were hiding in the ditch when Dad caught them.

Chapter 2

Years at the Eccher Place

Two miles north of Liberal, MO

After World War II, Dad had a chance to rent what was known as the Eccher section. I was five years old when we moved to the Eccher place.

A couple of times I thought my time bomb had exploded for sure. One time I was with Dad choring the cows when one cow decided to knock me down. I was lucky the manure was knee-deep and Dad was there to get her off.

The other time was when Dad had shocks of cane he would load up on a wagon pulled by the horses. When he would pick one up, there would be rats and mice under them. My job was to stomp them. All was going okay until a rat took off running. It was a big barn rat and I started chasing it. I was never blessed with great speed when running. Before long, the rat was chasing me! I can still see that big thing snapping its jaws and hear it barking. Yes, that rat barked! I thought the bomb was going off. Of course, Dad was laughing his head off.

After we moved to the Eccher place, we would all go to Liberal on Saturday night. I would go to the movie. It cost a dime. Roy Rogers and Gene Autry westerns were my favorite shows. One night the movie was "The Wizard of Oz." I got so scared! I didn't wet my pants, but I could have. To this day, I have never watched it again.

The town was so busy on Saturday night it was hard to find a place to park. The men would go to Lipscomb Feed Store and the women went to Jones Drug Store. Kids would run all over town. That's when I met my friend, Dennis "Dugan" Reed. I found out we were the same age and would be in the same class in school.

Dugan lived two miles north of us and we rode the same bus. The bus route was crazy. In the morning, I was the first one on and in the afternoon, I was the last one off. Great for a kid in first grade. Floyd Johnson was our bus driver and when we would get to the corner, the kids that got on first would yell, "North!" Once in a while, he would go north but not very often. The worst thing on that bus was a kid who was in the sixth grade named Frank Wolfenborger. He would make me scoot over and then sit by me. I thought he smelled like a horse that had been ridden hard and put away wet.

In the fall of that year, the school had a carnival. Each class had different games that parents and kids could play. Elementary classes were combined so there were only four classes in grade school and four in high school. That made eight different things to do. Along with games there were king and queen nominees from each grade. In the second grade, Nancy Rice and I won King & Queen for the grade school.

That's when I fell in love with Nancy. I just knew we would be married someday. I don't think she had the same feeling, so my romance didn't last long. No more girlfriends until High School.

In the third grade, we could carry cap guns and play cowboy and Indian at recess. There was a boy named Richard Dial in my class who was a fourth grader. He had failed one year, so he was actually two years older than me. Richard was always picking on me. He was my bully. One day at recess, he was calling me names and I had had enough. I took out my gun by the barrel and went after him. I woke up in Principal Barr's office. I don't know how I got there. Apparently, Richard had won the battle. Mr. Barr gave us both a paddling for fighting but that was the last of being bullied.

In the fourth grade, Ruth Wood (later married to Don Bunton) was my teacher. During that year she got ill and had to take some time off. Her mother took her place. Her name was Clara Wood. I loved Ruth but not so much her mother. She was very strict, and I don't think she ever smiled at school. One day at lunch break, I went out the northeast door of the gym which was on the back of the school. The school burned coal for heat and the janitors brought the cinders out to dump behind the school. That day Dennis Gilbert and Frank McKinney were throwing cinders at each other. They were far enough away from each other that they could get out of the way of incoming cinders. I said something to Frank. He turned his head toward me and didn't see the cinder Dennis had just launched. Unfortunately, the cinder hit him in the middle of his forehead cutting a big gash. Dennis disappeared very quickly. I went over to help Frank and heard someone pounding on the classroom window. It was Clara and she was convinced that I had thrown the cinder. I tried to tell her it wasn't me, but she didn't buy my story. So, an innocent kid got a spanking. My luck and the ticking got louder.

THIRD   AND   FOURTH GRADES

Miss Wood
Chester Bivans
Nancy Rice

Larry McColm
Phyllis White
Dennis Read
Sue Stevens

Kay Walker
Bob VanKirk
Nancy Essex
Tommy Crockett
Margaret McKinney

Bessie Lou Harvey
Dean Hoback
Elaine Thornton
Larry Lane
Barbara White

Betty Ann Vacca
Donald White
Shirley Crume
Roy Farmer
Erma Jo Riley

Kay Page
Mary Ruth Ryne
Robert Mitts
Terry Kocher
Shirley Travis

Ruby Aleshire
Richard Dial
Jackie Jackman
Don McColm
Lorena Suschnick

8

Chapter 3
Being a Hired Hand

In 1947, Dad bought a B Farmall tractor. That summer, he hired me to rake prairie hay. The pay was $1 per day and I made $6 that year.

All was going well until I decided to race Aunt Joan who was mowing. I didn't realize I was raking freshly mown hay which meant it wasn't cured enough to put in a windrow. I thought she was just waving at me! No, she was trying to stop me.

Once again being a slow runner, Dad could kick my butt on the go. I don't ever remember getting a spanking from him, but he could sure put that Number 10 where the sun don't shine.

Our hay baler at the time was a Case with a Wisconsin air-cooled motor. It took two guys to tie the bales. Dad hired Charlie and Clifford Hoover to do the baling. Charlie would run the shuttle and poke two wires through. Clifford would then tie them together.

One day, Clifford couldn't be there so Dad gave me the job of tying. That didn't work out because every time the plunger hit, the bale would move. I was slow and missed the eye on one end. By that time, I had two bales that needed tying. Trying hard to catch up, I crossed the wires and tied two bales together.

I got to go back to raking.

The next year I got to rake the whole summer and made enough money to buy a new Roy Rogers saddle and bridle out of the Sears & Roebuck catalog.

In 1950 my cousin Bob Crockett had taken over the raking, so Dad put me to discing the plowed ground on the Eccher place. It was in the north field with half mile rows. With an Allis WD and an eight-foot disc in second gear, it took forever to get anything done.

One day I figured out that if I would back the disc up and take the angle out to straighten the row, I could pull it in third gear and get a lot more done. BAD DEAL. I had made ridges every eight feet. There I went, running slow again. Never used third gear again.

After the Case baler Dad traded for a twine International. I was the tractor driver and Dad loaded the wagons. Once in a while it wouldn't tie a bale. I would stop while he would tie a square knot on it. One day he yelled to stop. I didn't hear him so when the hay hook came flying up by me, I stopped. He missed…probably on purpose.

The Little B

Chapter 4

My First Trip to Colorado

In 1947 or '48, Uncle Everett, Aunt Jean, Dad, Mom, my cousin Bob & I loaded up in our pickup. Dad put a tarp over the stock rack and that made it into a "camper." I remember seeing Pikes Peak for the first time when it was probably fifty miles away. That afternoon we started the drive up Pikes Peak. It was getting late so when we saw a wide place off the side of the road and thought it would make a good place to camp for the night, we stopped.

The next morning a car came flying by. Five minutes later another car came flying by. Then another and another. What was going on? Sometime later, we figured out they were racing to the top. We were camping on the racetrack! We had started up the mountain before they closed the road. Hoping the last car had gone by, we drove back down. Never made it to the top. The old International truck probably wouldn't have made it to the top anyway.

We went back to Denver where they had a big museum. It had bones of a woolly mammoth, dinosaurs, and all kinds of old animals. When we got there, Bob and I couldn't go in because there was fear that kids could catch Polio. Reminds me of COVID today. I guess skeletons are dangerous.

Chapter 5

The Year in Country School

In 1951, the people voted to consolidate the country schools. The little district that we lived in was Banner. There was still money in its operating fund, so they decided to open Banner school back up and not have to pay property tax that year. It didn't help my folks but it would save Mr. Starkey, our landlord, a little money. Our folks were okay with it because it would teach me and my little sister, Louise what it was like to walk to school every day. The school was a mile away from home and it was uphill both ways. A half mile from school there was a big hill, a quarter mile of mud road, a creek and then a big hill before we would get to school. It seemed like the road was always wet and muddy. The mud was clay and our boots weighed ten pounds each by the time we got to school. There was a house before we got to the first hill so we would ride our bikes and leave them there. Mom might have taken us a time or two but not very often.

Louise was in the second grade. There were three kids in her class. I was in the fifth grade and the only students were Betty Vacca and me. The teacher, Trula Frank, was from Jasper. I'm sure the pay was fantastic, so it had to be worth the drive.

That fall when I was ten and the farm work was finished, Uncle Everett and Aunt Jean planned a trip to San Diego to visit Jean's sister and family. They offered to take me and leave their daughter Sandra with my folks. Dad had bought a new Buick that year, so he loaned it to Everett to drive to California. It was the last of October. It started snowing when we started to go over Monarch Pass in Colorado. It was snowing so hard Everett could hardly see to drive. We came upon a grader that was going up the mountain. That was lucky, but it was going faster than we were. It soon disappeared. We kept going until the '51 Buick stopped going up. Then it started sliding back down the mountain. It turned sideways and started to go over the cliff. I don't know how far it was to the bottom but it was a long way. Everett hollered, "Jump!" All four doors flew open and we all jumped. Another ticking time bomb. Everett kept his foot on the brake and hand on the steering wheel. He was out of the driver's door hopping along side the car. Just before it went over, it stopped. What we hadn't seen was a ridge of snow that had been left by the grader. It had come down the mountain first before clearing the lane heading up. Praise God we were all okay.

The car was still sideways in the road when a big 6 x 6 Army truck with some deer hunters in it stopped to help. They were able to push the car back and turn it around so we could go back down the mountain. They asked Jean if she wanted to ride down with them. She took them up on their offer. When she got back into the car with us, she said she thought they had been drinking. The car might have been a better choice, she thought. We went to San Diego by way of El Paso.

As it turned out, that same snowstorm hit MO the next day and I didn't miss any school. Sometimes when people talk about big snowstorms they say, "Remember the one that came on Halloween?" No, we hit it the day before on Monarch Pass.

Louise reminded me of another snowstorm that winter. It started snowing midmorning and by afternoon it was getting pretty deep. Carl Truskett came in and told Miss Frank she had better let school out. As Louise and I were walking home, the snow was probably knee deep for me, making it considerably higher on Louise. She feared for her life. When we were half-way home, the Venable family invited us in for hot chocolate.

Mom had said to Dad that she was worried about us getting home. He met us at Venable's and got us home.

Chapter 6

Horses I Have Owned

Sundays always found us at Grandpa & Grandma Bunton's or Grandad Barney & Grandma Crockett's. On the Sundays we went to Irwin, Barney would get Sam, his workhorse, and put four of us cousins on him. We would just ride around the barn lot with Barney leading him. After Barney & Grandma moved to the town of Irwin, he gave Sam to Bob and me. I would keep Sam one week, then Bob kept him the next. We were living at the Eccher place and Bob at their place on Highway 43. It was a three-mile ride down the old silo road.

Couple of years later, Dad bought us a Welsh pony. She was bigger than a Shetland so an adult could ride her. She was a red and white paint. We named her Betsy. That was the same name Davy Crockett gave his rifle so that was how we came up with that name.

Tom at the Liberal May Day Parade

We had her bred to a Shetland. She had a little colt that we named Fury. A year later Fury was big enough to ride. I had been disking one morning and when I came in for lunch, Dad had put my Roy Rogers bridle and saddle on her and tied her up by the shop. I was about thirty yards from the house so I got on and rode her up to the house.

About that time Everett and Bob showed up and Bob said, "Let me ride! Let me ride!" When he got on, Fury said, "I don't think so!" and took off running and bucking. Bob stayed on until they got to the barn lot. That's when Bob came off the horse and landed in a fresh pile of cow manure face first. He got up spitting fresh cow poop. He said it tasted like lemon pie, his least favorite thing in the world. Bob took Fury home with him and she became his pony and I kept Betsy.

George Cox had a beautiful Palomino mare and had her bred to a stallion. I named that colt Cyclone. On my 13th birthday, Cyclone was big enough to ride so I saddled him up and climbed on. Like Bob, I should have waited until he was broken. He took off running and bucking north of the house down a steep hill. I didn't last long. I came off and landed on a rock. That was the first injury to my right shoulder. A pile of cow manure would have been softer. Just another time bomb.

Cyclone

Chapter 7
A Little Crockett History

One thing I enjoyed when we were over at Barney and Grandma's was listening to stories that Barney would tell.

One story was that when his dad, Samuel was in the Civil War, he was on a horse going west at a high rate of speed when he hit another rider going the opposite direction. Somehow his leg got tangled with the other rider. He was so severely injured that he was in bed for a year. Barney said that his dad was in pain the rest of his life.

When I think back, Samuel was my Great-Grandpa and he fought in the Civil War. Now I am a Great-Grandpa. How time has flown. Samuel died long before I was born, but I would have liked to have heard him tell the story.

When Barney was twelve, his family sold their farm in Blackwater, Mo. Barney's Uncle Robert lived in Texas, so they'd decided to load up a covered wagon and head to Texas.

When we rented the Eccher place Dad took everyone over to show his folks. After we went by the farm we went towards Liberal. When we went over the old bridge, Barney said, "I think we camped down there. Don't know if that was the place or not." If it was, one day his son would own the farm across the road on the other side of that old bridge.

When they went by Parsons, Kansas Barney said that when his dad was a young man, Samuel and two of his cousins came down to Parsons to settle. Samuel thought there were too many Indians, and he went back to Blackwater. His cousins stayed and had beautiful farms. When they went by on the way to Texas, his dad wouldn't even stop and say hello. Guess he was a little jealous and wished he had stayed. Uncle Paul and Aunt Betty Boles looked the place up and it was still in the family.

When they got to Caney, Kansas a guy met them and said that his farm was for sale. They went and looked at the farm and decided to buy it. On Monday morning they went to the farm and a man came out and said, "Can I help you?"

Samuel said that they'd bought the farm and had come to take possession. The man replied, "I don't think so because this is MY farm. By the way, I haven't seen my hired man for a couple of days."

Now they had lost all their money but still wanted to go to Texas. When Barney's grandson, Kenny Boles, started preaching in his first church, it was in Caney, Kansas. Barney wanted to hear him preach, but the memories of what happened there were still too great.

When they got into Oklahoma, there was a gun fight. Barney said that he and his dog hid under the covered wagon. He didn't know if it was robbers or the hired man that swindled them, but no one was hurt.

They got a little further on the way and then the horses got sick on alkali water. Broke, sick horses—it was time to go back home. To lighten the load, Samuel set his anvil and Civil War rifle out in the middle of the trail.

Uncle Everett asked Barney, "Why didn't you sneak back and get that rifle?"

Barney's answer was, "You didn't know my dad."

When they got back to Barton County, Missouri winter set in. They thought Barton County was great and that's why the Crockett's are in Barton County. Samuel had five boys and three girls so that's why there are so many Crockett's here.

Chapter 8

Cousins & Friends

Louise, Bobby & Tommy Crockett

One Sunday while we lived at the Eccher place, Mom had all the Crockett's over for dinner. Just north of the house was our chicken house with a big orchard around it. Louise and I and my cousins, Bob, Jerry, Kenny, and Jane were playing in the orchard when someone suggested that we should go gather the eggs in the chicken house. I got a bucket and everyone went to work. One row of the nests was taller than I was, so I reached up over my head to get the eggs. What I didn't realize was what I thought was an egg was really a black snake that had swallowed an egg. When I pulled my hand out, I had a snake! I don't know where I threw the snake, but hearts were pounding and kids were screaming. Mayhem had broken out.

I guess when we were all running out the door, somehow the door hit a yellow jacket nest. I think we all got nailed. Then we were crying for real. That was the last time anyone wanted to gather eggs.

None of my Bunton cousins lived close by. When we went over to Grandpa & Grandma Bunton's I would take my friend, Don Bainter with me. We both liked to fish and Grandpa had three nice ponds. Grandpa had a place where he had what he called sod worms. These worms were ten to twelve inches long so we had plenty of bait. If we caught a small bass, we had to throw it back so it could grow. Hardly ever caught a bass big enough to keep. We could keep all the perch and bullheads we caught. Grandpa would have us use cane poles to fish with, but sometimes when he didn't go with us, we would sneak out his bait casting rods to use. Always would get a backlash we couldn't untangle. Then Grandpa would come yelling, "You, Rummies! I'll dust your britches!" Never did, but he sure yelled.

Grandma & Grandpa Bunton's Farm, west of Verdella, MO

Tom & Don Bainter   Great-Aunt Etta Wagner
Tom & Louise

Louise Crockett and Barney Crockett
Kenny Boles, Bob Crockett, Tom, & Jerry Boles

Tommy Crockett, Bobby Crockett, Jane Quackenbush
and an unnamed goat, Irwin, Mo

Crockett Cousins

(Front) Kathy Crockett
(Middle) Sandy Crockett, Kenny Boles, Louise Crockett
(Back) Jerry Boles, Jane Quackenbush, Bob Crockett, Tom

Bunton Cousins

Sandy Reeves, Marilyn Reeves, Linda Bunton,
Kathy Crockett, Louise Crockett
Kenny Reeves, Richie Reeves, Brad Thomas,
Randy Thomas, Tom Crockett, Larry Bunton

Chapter 9
Hunting

Putt McClendon lived ½ mile south of us when we lived on the Eccher place. His house was at the bottom of a steep hill. Bob and I would take the Little B tractor, kick it into neutral, and see how far we could coast. Then other times we would take our bikes and see who could coast the farthest.

One day I saw Putt outside and I stopped to ask him if he would teach me how to squirrel hunt. He said, "Yes, come on down." Dad gave me a little .22 short rifle that was just a single shot. After shooting, you had to take out your pocketknife and scrape out the empty shell. That would take a little time so if you missed, the squirrel would be long gone. One time Putt told Dad, "Tommy can't hit a sitting squirrel but if the squirrel is running, he can hit it in the head."

After we moved, I bought a .22 Marlin from our preacher, Wesley Arrington. The problem with it was that it wouldn't let the clip go down far enough to get another cartridge. So, you had to push the clip down with your thumb. There again: you miss/squirrel gone.

If I got home from school and had enough time, I would walk down to Putt's and get his two dogs. They were good squirrel dogs and would tree them for me. It was usually dark when I would get back home. I would have to clean the squirrel with a flashlight. Mom would chicken-fry them and I thought they were delicious. Of course, Mom could make anything taste good.

One winter, Cousin Kenny Reeves was visiting when we had enough snow that school was cancelled. We decided to go rabbit hunting. There was a big briar patch on the back of our place. We took a gunnysack just in case we got some rabbits. Rabbits were plentiful and before we knew it, we had a sack full.

It was a mile hike back to the house and a sack full of rabbits made going real slow. It was almost dark, so we went to the barn to clean them. On the first rabbit I cut myself, so Dad had to help Kenny with the rabbits. Dad wasn't a happy camper.

In the fourth grade, Oskaloosa closed its school. We had a new classmate named John Rawlings. John and I became best friends and are still friends today. We had about the same athletic skills so in a race there was someone I could keep up with.

One day John Rawlings asked me to come over to his house after school to spend the night and go rabbit hunting on Saturday. Of course, you need a gun to rabbit hunt so I took my little .22 and got on the bus.

Our bus driver said, "I don't know about this. I guess if you leave it up front with me it will be ok."

Try that today and you would be locked up and the keys thrown away. As I remember, we didn't get any rabbits but had a lot of fun.

Chapter 10

I Thought Mom Should Know

In the old days when a couple got married, all the neighbors would go to their house and chivaree them. Most of the time it was all in fun. One night we went to Rubin & Tootsie Smith's. Rubin was in his fifties and Tootsie was in her forties. It was all a surprise on them but they knew it would happen sometime, so they had candy & cigars to pass out.

I was outside when I heard something up in the tree. I turned around and there she was. My Aunt Joan and her friend Patty Sechrist were up in that tree smoking cigars. I couldn't believe it! Not my Aunt Joan! I had to stop this.

I ran into the house where Mom was yelling, "You have to come quick because Joan is smoking a cigar!"

Mom was mortified....NOT with Joan, but with ME. Mom said I should have minded my own business and not embarrassed her in front of all those women.

Another interesting fact about the Smith's was that they had the first television set that I knew of in all of Barton County. We would sometimes go there to watch a show. The nearest station broadcasting at that time was in Kansas City.

KOAM from Pittsburg began broadcasting in 1953. We got our own television set and would sit in front of it watching the test pattern until the broadcast day began at 5:00 p.m.

Tubes in the old sets would burn out frequently. Fortunately, our neighbor Little Bill Curless set up a repair shop in a building in his backyard. We'd haul the TV up to him and if he didn't have the tube he needed, he would pick it up the next time he went to Pittsburg.

Chapter 11
Wooly Buck Ranch

The Eccher place was actually owned by John Starkey of Illinois. Herb and Hazel Eccher thought that the U.S. would go back to the Depression after the war and they didn't want to live on the farm. That wasn't the way things went and the economy took off. Ecchers said they would like to have the farm back but Dad said, "No," he would like to continue renting it. Starkey had claimed he couldn't sell the farm but that wasn't the truth because he soon sold it to Herb and Ed Eccher.

Dad & Mom and Uncle Jim & Aunt Dorothy Bunton had planned a trip to Florida. I begged to go with them. Now I don't know if everyone was good with that idea, but I did get to go. It was during the school year and I would miss some school. There was a snowstorm while we were gone and it turned out that once again I didn't miss any school at all.

When we got back home, Uncle Everett said we were going to have to move. It seems that the very night Mom had fed Starkey biscuits and gravy and he said the land was tied up in an estate settlement, he went to town and sold the farm. In an ironic turn of events, Dad bought the place where Wilma & I now live from Herb Eccher.

Dad looked at different places to buy near Irwin, but nothing seemed to work out. Going to Liberal one day, he saw a place for sale just a half mile south of the Eccher place. It was made up of pasture, hay meadow, brush and briers, but not tillable soil. He found out it was owned by Bill Curless. They called it the "Wooly Buck Ranch." There had been a Boy Scout Camp on it at one time. The Boy Scout building had been destroyed by a tornado.

When Dad bought the Wooly Buck there was no house or barn there. He hired Willy Bowman to build the house. Dad helped Willy when he could. Mom was pregnant that summer but it didn't slow her down from painting and varnishing every room as it was completed.

Dad and Jim McClendon dug the basement with scoops on the back of their tractors. Dad was going to form the inside walls and use the dirt on the outside for the forms. There was a rain before the walls were poured and the East wall collapsed. Dad used some old railroad ties for the outside.

One morning before church, Mom was walking across the kitchen in her high heel shoes when one heel went through the linoleum. Not long after, Aunt Jean also had a heel go through. Termites had gotten in the old railroad ties and then started eating through the kitchen floor. I got the job of digging up the old ties every day after school and then treating the ground.

Dad told me if anything ever happened to him to sell the place fast. That's the one thing he asked that I never did. Guess he thought we would let it go back to brush and briers.

If Dad could see the place today, I think he would be very proud. Keith has a big pond and cabin east of the house where all the family and friends get together for swimming and fishing.

Before we moved into the new house, Kathy Sue was born on November 5, 1952. We had to be off the Eccher place by March, so we moved in February 1953.

Louise, Walter, Kathy, Marjorie & Tom
at Grandpa & Grandma Bunton's House 1953

Chapter 12

Highway Driving

My folks had become good friends with Paul & Mildred Davis who went to the Methodist Church with us. They played cards together every week. Paul mentioned to Dad that he was behind in planting his soybeans. It would help if someone could disc while he planted. So, Dad loaned me out to help Paul. I packed up and stayed with Paul for two weeks. Mildred was away so Paul and I "batched" the two weeks. Paul milked cows by hand and I would carry each bucket of milk up to the windmill and put it in a cream can.

Paul had a new Ford N8 tractor with a mounted disc. I thought that sure beat a WD Allis. I stayed in 2nd gear. After we got his place planted, Paul needed to go plant his dad's beans. His dad lived four miles northeast of Lamar. Paul loaded his Ford tractor onto his truck to take it to his dad's. His folks were not home, and we needed a way back to Paul's on Highway 43. Paul asked me if I thought I could follow him in his pickup truck. Sure, no problem! Any eleven-year-old could drive a truck to Lamar. The only thing I worried about was the stop and turn onto Highway 71. Made it just fine, no trouble and no cops.

Chapter 13

Boy Scouts

When I went back to Liberal School in the sixth grade, Gladwyn Gold was the new Superintendent of Schools. Mr. Gold started a new Boy Scout troop. Most of the boys in grade school joined. We did a lot of camping trips, mostly not too far from Liberal.

Mr. Gold was from McDonald County and knew a good place to camp there. The place was hard to get to, but it was beautiful. Story was that a Jessie James movie was filmed there. Big Sugar Creek ran through the farm. It was clear and cold, especially in the spring. Lee Sprenkle was also from that area and he drove the bus full of boys there.

Dad offered to take our truck, so all the camping gear was loaded in our old '49 Chevy. Uncle Everett had an Army tent that could hold four cots. Dad and I put it up. Mr. Gold and Lee slept with us.

There was a one-store town about two miles south of our camping spot. It was named Cyclone. It was probably put there for the movie because the store was the one and only thing around.

One day some of us decided to walk there and buy some candy and pop. When we got back, some of the boys came running out and said to me, "Your dad saved David Lane's life!"

David had Epilepsy. When he went into swim in that cold water, he had a seizure. Dad jumped in and pulled him out. David recovered quickly and was fine the rest of the camp out. I had seen David have some of those episodes at school and they were very scary.

One other camping trip, the troop went down east of Joplin on a creek bank. It was cold and rainy. Dad again hauled the camping gear, but this time he went over to the nearby fertilizer plant to haul a load of fertilizer home. He didn't waste any time that way.

The next morning, Mr. Gold and Rodney Overman were going over something in the Boy Scout handbook. All of a sudden, Rodney threw the book in my face and went to screaming. I didn't know what was going on. Quickly, Mr. Gold tackled Rodney and went to pounding on his pant leg. What Rodney didn't realize was that he was standing on the old campfire from the night before and the hot coals had set his pant leg on fire. Rodney was hurt pretty badly and had to go to the hospital. Luckily, Mr. Gold was there and put the fire out. It was all over before I knew what was going on. Even if I had known, I wouldn't have been able to tackle Rodney or put the fire out.

One day Mr. Gold had some of us demonstrate some different skills we had learned at a school assembly. My part was to show how to tie a new knot. I thought it would be funny to show how to tie a hangman's noose.

After my great presentation, I could tell Mr. Gold was not impressed. Guess he didn't think school kids needed to know how to tie a hangman noose. You never know.

Chapter 14

Church Camp

In the summer of 1953, I got invited to go to the Hannon Church camp. Cousin Bob said that he was going so he wanted me to go with him. The group that went was Bob, Sue Weaver, Anita Coiner and me. The camp was east of Springfield near the town of Niangua, MO.

Bob and I got put in a cabin with boys from St. Louis. Country boys and big city boys didn't have too much in common. One of their plans for the week was to go out in the rocks and timber to catch Copperhead and Rattlesnakes and milk the poison in a jar. They were going to sell it for a lot of money. Thankfully, we never found any snakes.

Don't ever try this at home. They would make each other pass out by pressing on the main artery in the neck that gets oxygen to the brain. One boy, Danny liked it so much that after he came to, he wanted to get knocked out again. I don't remember how many times he passed out, but way too many.

One night they loaded him in an ambulance and took him to the hospital. That night at the church service, we all went to the altar to pray for him. I never heard what the outcome was. I'm sure it couldn't have been good to cut off the blood supply to his brain over and over. No one ever played that game again.

Outside of that, nothing else exciting happened that week. I got a letter from Mom telling me how many jars of green beans she had canned that week so we were going to eat good that winter.

Recently I asked Dr. Ko about that boy getting knocked out so many times. He said if he regained consciousness quickly, as young as he was, it probably didn't cause any permanent damage. Hope so.

Chapter 15

The Day I Saw a Miracle

Floyd & Ray Banwart did custom silo filling. There was a silo on the Eccher place we still used and they also helped fill silos for Grandpa, Uncle Frank Bunton and Uncle Jim Bunton that summer.

When we got to Jim's silo, the Banwarts had to go to a funeral. So Dad, along with Everett, Don Smith & Harold Smith and I, decided to put up the pipe from the blower and the down spout. We would have that much out of the way. A solid pipe was used on the outside of the silo and flexible sections were used on the inside. Someone would have to be on top of the silo to hook up a block and tackle to pull it up. Dad volunteered to go up on top. After the outside was up, we needed to put the down sections together. Someone had the bright idea that instead of using the rod on top of the silo, we could put the block and tackle on the spout that was on the fill tube. It seemed like a good idea. I was on a step ladder and would hook up the sections as the guys pulled them up. Dad was standing up leaning on the spout cross-legged. BOOM! Everything came crashing down.

Aunt Dorothy, who was watching from the outside, started screaming. Somebody yelled, "Walt's gone!" I looked up and Dad's straw hat came floating down.

Everett, Don, and Harold were pushing each other out of the way trying to get out of the silo. I was numb. Couldn't move. Didn't want to see my dad splattered on the ground.

Finally, I went out and everyone was looking up. There was Dad, still on top of the silo hanging by one pant leg upside down. He was swinging back and forth trying to get hold of the top of the silo. Definitely not out of the woods yet.

After what seemed like an eternity, he was able to grab the top of the silo and pull himself up. Aunt Dorothy always said he climbed up by his fingernails. His time bomb was ticking. The rod on top of the silo had poked a hole in his overalls and the cuff didn't tear off. Thinking about that for a long time, the only way I can explain how that rebar made a hole in his overalls is that the rebar must have been up inside his pant leg. When he fell, the rebar pierced its way out.

Only a miracle of God saved him that day. Kathy was just a baby. Had he been killed our lives would have been changed forever. On our way home Dad said, "Don't tell your mom about today."

I didn't tell Mom, but Aunt Dorothy told her every detail. Some people said Walt sure was lucky. Luck didn't have a thing to do with it. Of all the things that had to go right, the odds would have been a million to one. The rebar had to be sharp enough to poke a hole in his overalls. He had to be standing in the right place. He had to fall the right direction. The straps didn't break or come unhooked on the bibs. The cuff had to be strong enough not to rip off with a two-hundred-pound man falling, then swinging back and forth.

Evidently, when the men had bolted the gooseneck together, someone had used the wrong bolts or didn't put all the bolts in the joint. The next day, Dad let Ray Banwart go on top.

With Dad's close brush with death, he started talking with Louise and me about the need to give our hearts to the Lord and be saved. One Sunday night we did just that. That's the only time I saw my Dad cry with joy.

One time later, I heard Aunt Dorothy say she just wished she could see God. Maybe she didn't see God, but she sure had seen Him at work.

Chapter 16
Learning How to Swim

My Dad would take me down to the pond and throw me in. I would swim back and he would throw me in again. Swim back and throw me in. Swimming was the easy part. Getting out of the gunnysack was the hard part....Okay, I can have a little fun with this book. Lighten up!

Sometimes our family wanted to have a fish fry. Uncle Jim Bunton had a gill net (illegal) and we would all go down to one of our ponds on the Eccher place. In the southeast quarter, there was a prairie meadow with three ponds in a row. The north pond was the newest and deepest. As the men pulled the sein, some fish would try to jump over it. We kids would go behind and try to stop the fish from jumping. I got a little too far out and went in over my head. It was sink or swim. I made it back, but it wasn't very pretty.

One summer I went to Boy Scout camp. They had a little lake to swim in. To be able to swim in the lake, you had to show the guys in charge that you could actually swim. When asked if I could swim, I shook my head no. They told me to go over to a little wading pool. Some of the boys were laughing at me so I went back and told them that I *could* swim. To prove myself, I had to swim thirty yards across the lake. They had a walkway that went across the lake. There was a guy with a pole you could grab onto if you couldn't make it. I made it but splashed a lot of water. No one could laugh now.

Chapter 17

Global Warming

In 1954 there was global warming. I don't care if the ding-bat weathermen say it never got to 121 degrees, I was there. They weren't. At least it was in Rubin Smith's prairie hay meadow on July 15th. The hay was so short and dry you could hook the rake onto the mower.

Cows weren't going to have much to eat that winter. Dad and Everett would go out in the morning and cut corn with knives and load up our pickup with the stock rack on it. That evening I would drive the truck and Dad would throw out the corn. That was better than what the grasshoppers had to eat. The hedge post would be covered with grasshoppers eating the bark off the posts.

We didn't have air conditioning and it would still be 100 degrees at night. A fan didn't do you any good. The folks would take a mattress out on the front porch at night to sleep on. We all slept on one mattress. One night when I laid down, I didn't see that I was laying on a blister bug. That was not good. We survived.

In the spring of 1956, Rudy Schriener called Dad. He said if we would trade for a John Deere hay baler, we could do some custom baling for him. Dad took him up on it and that summer we started baling what is now part of the Prairie State Park. Rudy liked our work and before we were done that summer, we had baled 800 acres of prairie hay. We baled it every year until Rudy died in 1972.

This was a whole new ballgame. We needed another tractor and mower so Dad bought a little C Allis and a John Deere seven-foot sickle mower that went along with our H Farmall with an International seven-foot mower. We also did away with wagons and used a sled which was made of four twenty-foot 2x12 oak boards.

Bob & I mowed. Louise raked. Dad and Everett did the baling. Brown and Red Percy along with Willy VanDorn hauled the hay with our 1949 Chevy truck. Brown took both doors off the truck to make it easier to get in and out, plus it would be cooler. After they would get loaded and roped on, they would jump down on the cab, then the fender, then onto the ground. Before the summer was over the top of the cab looked like it had two wash tubs on it. After that summer, the old '49 got scrapped out and put in the draw behind my house. It's still there.

After we finished baling that summer, Dad traded our old '51 Buick for a new Chevrolet Bel-Air. It was kind of yellow, kind of green two-toned. Chevy never used that paint again after '56. Didn't have a radio in the dash but I put a radio in the trunk with a speaker by the rear window. It was turned on with a switch under the dash. You couldn't change stations, but you didn't need to if it was on WHB Rock & Roll from Kansas City. That wasn't my folks' favorite station, but it was mine. Rock & Roll was much different in '56 than it is today.

Tom & the '56 Chevy

Chapter 18

A Story About Dad

John Post owned a pasture across the road from my corral at Bronaugh. We would sometimes visit when we happened to be at our pastures at the same time.

John would tell me the story about when he and Dad went to the Methodist Church Annual District Meeting. He represented the Bronaugh church and Dad went from Liberal. In the late 50's we had a preacher at the Methodist Church who just wasn't very well liked by the congregation. The District Superintendent said he was going to send the same preacher back to Liberal for the next year.

Dad said, "That preacher won't stay."

The Superintendent said, "Oh yes, he wants to come back."

To which Dad replied, "No, he won't stay because I'm the treasurer and I won't write him a check. He won't stay."

"Okay then, I will get someone else to go to Liberal."

John told me that story ten times. He thought Dad was pretty sharp. He died laughing every time he told it.

Chapter 19

High School

In high school, John Rawlings and I both went out for basketball. Didn't make the team. That spring we went out for baseball. Didn't make the team. Liberal didn't have football when we were in school. Coach said that if the school had a football team, we would be on it. Talent gone to waste.

One day in Phys. Ed., we were playing basketball. As I was running down the court, I turned around and my eye ran into Robert Hall's thumb. I hit the floor and the first thing I remember hearing was Mr. Barr saying, "Everyone stand back because when he gets up, he will be swinging." I guess he still remembered me and Richard Dial.

In the fall each year our FFA class had a Barnwarming where you took your date for games and square dancing. For refreshments we had apple cider and potato chips.

My freshman year, I asked Jill Workman to go to the Barnwarming with me, but she said no. Square dancing without a girl is not much fun, but the apple cider was good.

The next year for Barnwarming, I asked Alta Dukes if she would go with me if I could get the car. I was sure she would say no, but she said yes. Now I had to talk Dad into letting me borrow the car. I was only 15 and had no driver's license. Alta lived in Iantha. He said yes, so I was set. After we danced the night away, we went up to Jones Drug Store. I guess we didn't have enough apple cider and potato chips. When we left the Drug Store and started to Iantha, the old Six Cylinder took off a little too fast and the nightwatchman started yelling. I was toast! No driver's license. He'd probably put me in jail.

"I saw you Jay-driving," he said.

"No, I was parked on the East side of Main Street."

Alta backed me up, but my fun night was over. I just knew Dad would hear about me speeding on Main and that wouldn't be good. If he ever heard about it, he never mentioned it.

The next summer I finally turned sixteen and could get my driver's license. The next Saturday I asked Dad if Bob, Jerry Boles and I could borrow the car and go to Pittsburg to go swimming. He said, "You ought to take some girls."

I said, "Oh, there are girls in Pittsburg." As luck would have it, there were some girls! When we got done swimming and driving around the park, Bob said, "Hey, the girls in that car are waving at us." We waved back.

We followed them to where one of them lived. We stopped and talked. One of the girls was named Jean Workman, the other was Nelly Snekenboger. They had stopped at Jean's house. I asked Jean for her telephone number and she gave it to me. So Dad, there *are* girls in Pittsburg.

One Saturday night I didn't have anything to do so I decided I would call up Jean and maybe go out to a movie. When I called, she answered. I said, "This is Tom Crockett. We met last summer." Then I said, "How are you… (then for some stupid reason I added the word) …feeling?"

When she stopped laughing, she said, "Okay." What a way to ask a girl out. I went by her house and talked but never went out with her. She probably thought "what a dork."

After that dating disaster in Pittsburg, it was time to move on, lick my wounds and get over it. Next, I asked Sue Weaver if she would like to go to a movie. She said yes, and when I went to pick her up her dad, Everett, was sitting at the kitchen table. He never turned around or spoke.

I thought, "Okay, I don't know what I ever did to you." Made me feel good about taking his daughter out. We went out again and the same thing happened. He didn't look up or speak. Everett's sister was my Great-Aunt Dorothy Bunton so it wasn't like he didn't know me.

Time to move on with this dating game. I went out with a lot of different girls, but it was usually only once. I don't know: was it me or them?

One Saturday night John Rawlings and I decided to go to Pittsburg to go roller skating. There was a roller-skating rink above the old Buick building and it was always full of kids. The rink had different types of skates, one of them was Ladies' Choice. Someone tapped me on the shoulder. When I turned around there was the most gorgeous, beautiful girl I had ever seen. She asked me to skate. I froze! Went numb! Like the stupid idiot that I was, I shook my head "no!" So she asked John and he skated with her.

Here I'd gone to Pittsburg to meet girls and I had blown it. I asked John what her name was and he said, "I think it was Wilma. I don't remember her last name."

I kicked myself all the way home. Wonder what would have happened if I had only said yes.

In my senior year of high school, I took Algebra. Wayne Vacca was our teacher. It was Wayne's first year of teaching so he was learning along with the rest of us. Nancy Rice, who would become the Valedictorian of our class, was the person I chose to sit by so she could help me. I think she knew more than Mr. Vacca.

One day I asked if she would like to go to a movie. She said yes, so we went to Lamar to see a movie. We had a great time. When we got back to her house, I turned the car lights off. Two minutes later, the porch light came on, then went off, then came on again.

Nancy said, "I guess Mom wants me to go in." Unlike Everett Weaver her mom spoke to me when I picked Nancy up.

I thought maybe there was still a little spark from the second grade. "Would you like to go out next Saturday night?"

"No, my old boyfriend, Tommy Myers is coming home from college for Thanksgiving and I want to go out with him."

Another one and done. That spark just went out. I guess because I was throwing water on it.

One day John Rawlings asked me if I would ask Judy Butterfield out to double date with him and Jody Irwin. She said, "Sure." We went to Nevada to a movie.

Another Saturday night, I went out with Judy to a drive-in movie in Pittsburg. After we parked, I noticed Ronnie VanKirk was parked next to us. I thought that girl with him looked familiar. When Ronnie and I walked up to the concessions stand, I asked, "Who are you with tonight?"

He replied, "It's Wilma McCabe."

When it was time for our senior prom, I asked Judy to go with me. She said she would like to. After the prom, it started raining about the time we got back to Judy's house. We sat and talked the rest of the night.

Our class was leaving the next morning on our senior trip to Rockaway Beach. The bus was leaving Liberal at 6 a.m. I got home in time to get my suitcase and catch the bus.

After school was out, I went out with Judy a couple more times. When we got back to her house, I asked her if she would like to go steady. She said "yes", so I gave her my class ring. I finally had a steady girl. I told her I would be back the next Saturday night.

When I went up to the door, she met me and said, "I am breaking up with you and here is your class ring back." Okay, at least I had a steady girl one week.

That summer I would go into Liberal on Saturday night and meet up with some of my old classmates. They would want to go out and drink beer. I didn't drink so I would go back home.

"You sure don't stay out late anymore," Mom said. Nothing to do.

One Saturday night later that summer, I met the guys in town. I told them that I was going to the skating rink in Pittsburg and "...if Wilma McCabe is there, she is mine so you can all back off."

Wilma *was* there and this time I *did* skate with her. The rink closed up at 10 and I asked Wilma if I could take her home. She said, "My mom is waiting for me, but I will go ask." Her mom said it was okay, so I got to take her home.

After we were on our way, she said she lived on 13th street but it didn't go all the way through to Broadway so I should turn at a certain house, go two blocks north and then east again. I wondered, "Can I ever remember how to get to her house again?"

I walked her to the door and asked her if she would go out the next Saturday night? She said yes and gave me a sweet goodnight kiss. I fell in love with that first kiss. When I got home, I said to myself, "Now I know who I am going to marry." We hadn't gone on a real date yet, but somehow it was going to work out. We went out a few more times and then I asked her if she would like to go steady. She said, "Yes."

Chapter 20
College Years

That fall I decided to go to Pitt State in Pittsburg (then called Kansas State College of Pittsburg.) I didn't want to drive back and forth from home; besides I didn't own a car. Leroy Gribble was in my class at Liberal and he said he was going to Pitt too, "So why don't we room together?" That sounded good to me, so we got a room in the dorm. Our room was on the third floor in Trout Hall. It didn't take long to meet new friends.

I would go home every weekend and Mom would wash all my dirty clothes. When I went back on Sunday night, she would send a fried chicken and an apple pie. I got to eat good for a couple of days. Other nights there were a couple of boys that had cars so we would load up and go to Argentine's Italian Restaurant on the North end of Broadway.

Wilma said that her grandparents, Jim & Bessie McCabe lived just south of Argentine's and there was a dirt racetrack on the south side of them. I told her, "I remember going to the car races with Uncle Everett at that track. I remember seeing a bunch of people on the garage roof watching the race for free."

She said, "Yes, that was me and my folks." We had been in close contact back when we were still in grade school!

Back at the dorm after we got all our homework out of the way, we would play cards, of course. Usually, it was penny ante poker. You didn't get rich, but you didn't lose any money.

Now don't try this at home. One night the card game was down the hall in Jim Gosh's room. The room was full, so I was with Big Don Kimbrel in his room. I noticed some cherry bombs, so I cut the bottom off one.

I dumped the powder in an ash tray. I wondered what would happen if we lit it. Big Don smoked so he used his cigarette lighter and there was a big flash. I was looking at the empty cherry bomb and said, "Let's have some fun. Let's go down to where the big card party is going on. You crack the door and I'll light the empty bomb and throw it in the room."

I lit that cherry bomb and threw it. We took off running. Guys started screaming, cards and money went flying.

Hey, it was just a joke. Nothing happened, but the guys didn't think it was very funny. Since Big Don and I were the only ones not playing cards, it wasn't too hard to figure out the guilty ones. Just a joke, guys. Get over it!

One night I borrowed Big Don's car and went to Wilma's house. When I got back to the dorm, I looked up at my room on the third floor. My window was open and there on a ledge that was about four foot down and three foot wide was everything in my room. My bed, my desk, books, clothes—they didn't forget anything. I got paid back big time.

I got my clothes and books back in, but it looked like I was going to have to sleep on the ledge. After they had their fun, they helped me get it all back in. Sometimes jokes have consequences.

Outside of the skills I gained in my Communication Classes, I haven't used much of anything else I took in college. But I do think my first year in the dorm helped me grow up.

Along with Big Don Kimbrel, his roommate Ray Sprigg was a good friend of mine. They lived across the hall from Leroy and me. We went out to eat together, played cards, and spent a lot of time just shooting the bull. After we got out of class in June 1960, I never saw either one of them again.

One day in about 2013 or so, I was looking up someone's obituary online when I came across one of a woman from Bronson, Kansas. Her last name was Sprigg. That got my interest, so I read on down. It listed a son named Ray who lived in Thornton, Colorado. I did some searching online, got his address and dropped him a letter and he answered. He said he still had an aunt and uncle who lived in Nevada, MO and was coming for a visit.

One evening he called and suggested we meet at a restaurant in Nevada. When Wilma and I pulled up, there were two guys standing outside but I didn't recognize either one, so I drove on past. I didn't see anyone else around though so I decided that must have been Ray. It had only been fifty-three years since I had seen him. He had gotten older.

Ray's wife, Sharon, and son were with him on the trip but his wife wasn't feeling well so we didn't get to meet her. We had a lot of catching up to do on the things that had happened over all those years. We ended the visit with Ray's plan to come back to Nevada when we could talk more.

Ray's wife came down with an illness that forced him to stay in Colorado to take care of her. She has since passed away. One of his sons now works just west of St. Louis. When Ray was on his way home from visiting him, he came by our place to visit a couple of times. When Wilma and I go to Colorado in the summer of 2023, we plan to meet Ray and catch up on more old times.

Chapter 21

A Wild Ride

As I drove by the Crawford County State Park recently, I remembered an incident that happened with Wilma and me on a double date with John Rawlings and Jody Irwin. It made me think of an old song by Jimmy Dean: "Big Bad John." I've changed some of the words of the song to fit the situation of that night.

Big, Bad Tom

He didn't say much, kind of quiet and shy.
If you spoke at all, you'd just say "hi"
To Tom, Big Bad Tom.

Now one bright moonlit night after the drive-in show
To the park to do some sparkin' they would go.
The park was full of roads and old strip-pits.
To keep from gettin' lost, you had to use your wits.
All was going well on that night of nights
When all of a sudden came bright headlights.
Someone yelled, "They are chasing us!"
At least that someone knew not to cuss.
Girls started crying, hearts beat fast.
Everyone thought they'd breathed their last.
Except Tom. Big Bad Tom.

Tom, it is told, said with a grin
"Hang on, gang. We are in for a spin."
With nerves of steel and a foot of lead,
Off to the races they all sped.
Tom turned out the lights; raced the rest of the way

In that old icky-colored Fifty-Six Chevrolet.
Through the dust and dirt that scary night
Tom turned left and they turned right.
Brave Tom. Big Bad Tom.

Now they've closed that road to the worthless pit
And even put a heavy iron gate across it.
We'll never know what those bad boys were up to
But it was the Good Lord that seen 'em through
With Tom. Big Bad Tom.

Chapter 22

True Love

In the summer of 1960, Wilma and I had been going together for a year. One night I asked if she would like to get engaged. She said yes!

I told her, "Tomorrow we can go over to Coffeyville where my Uncle Paul Boles and cousin Jerry have a jewelry store. That way you can get the ring you want and I can get a discount." Jerry helped her pick out a ring and now we were engaged.

In the fall, I went back to Pitt with Don Bainter as my roommate. That year I had my own car, a 1956 Mercury. Nighttime would find me in Rosie's kitchen, that was Wilma's mother. None of my old friends from the year before were back so the dorm was just a place to sleep.

By Christmas time we had been engaged long enough. I said, "Let's get married."

I didn't have a job, a house, or any money, but we were in love and that's all that mattered. School wasn't out until the last of January but we could get married over Christmas break.

On December 22, 1960, we were married in the Methodist Church in Liberal. We had a big wedding with my folks and two sisters and her folks and two sisters plus the preacher, Alan Finley.

I thought with all the time we have until we need to be back, why don't we go to New Orleans on our honeymoon? So we got married, went back to the folk's house to have cake that Rosie brought and strawberry pop for punch that Mom came up with in a pinch, having believed me when I said we weren't going to have a reception.

Tom & Wilma McCabe Crockett
Wedding Reception at Tom's Parent's Home

Then off to New Orleans we went. I don't know what we thought we would do there. The first day I said, "Let's go down to Bourbon Street." We were driving down a big street but when we got to where we needed to turn, no left turns were allowed. I turned right and WOW, not the nicest part of town. It was Christmas Eve and the streets were full of people having a good time.

Because we were the only white people in a 1956 Mercury, I said, "Lock your door and let's get out of here!" We made it back to our motel. That was enough excitement for one day.

The next day was Christmas. We found a little zoo that had some talking parrots. After that we stopped and looked at a brochure trying to find something else to do. While sitting there, a big black limo pulled up. A guy got out and asked if we would like to take a tour of the town. I didn't know if this was legit. About that time, two boys pulled up and got in with him so I decided it must be okay and we got in the limo.

The first place we went was a cemetery. I knew it! We were going to be robbed and killed. But no, he was just showing us that the city was below sea level so every grave was above ground. We toured the French Quarter and drove down Bourbon Street. Then he took us back to our car. We didn't get robbed *or* killed.

We had had about enough of New Orleans, so we headed north. That night we got a motel room and Wilma said, "I believe I'll go take a bath."

All of a sudden, I heard a scream. When I went in, she had accidentally turned on the shower and soaked her hair. I made a big mistake and laughed. She wasn't a very happy camper. I thought I was going to have to sleep on the couch on my honeymoon.

We left home as a couple, but we came home as a family. Now I needed to figure out what I wanted to do for the rest of my life.

I told Dad that History was my favorite subject but outside of teaching, what else could you do with a History degree? I told him that I would like to come back and farm. He said he thought that would be a good idea. He knew that Donnie & Irene Thomas had bought a place and when they moved, we could rent Jack Thornton's uncle's house where they had been living. Rent was $10 a month but truthfully, that was a little too high for the shape the house was in.

After growing up in town, farm life was something that took a while for Wilma to get used to. The old 1956 Mercury found its way to Pittsburg quite often.

Chapter 23
The Last of the '56 Chevy

In the summer of 1961, we had been baling hay when the baler broke down. Dad went home to get the car to go for parts. Mom told him that the kids at school had a car wash to raise money for their class. She had taken the car in and left it there. Dad called the school and asked them to bring the car back home.

Cork Walker's family lived in the house south of the folks. Kathy had ridden her bike to Walker's that morning to play with her friend, Corkie. When it was time for Kathy to go home, Corkie had ridden down the first hill with her. They parted company and Corkie was about halfway back up their hill and Kathy was halfway up the north hill towards the drive into the cedar trees. Just then Mike Savage came flying down the road in our '56 Chevy. Seeing Corkie on the east side of the road, he swerved to the other lane, then he overcorrected and went into the east ditch. Over correcting again, the car flipped and landed upside down in the west ditch. Kathy remembers thinking that driver isn't being safe, seeing nothing but dust. By the time the dust cleared, Mike was out of the car and walking up the hill to Walker's. That was when it hit her that it was *our car*. She pedaled home as fast as she could, threw the bike down in the yard and ran screaming to the house. She was crying so hard, they didn't know what had happened.

Dad didn't have any collision insurance and the car was a total loss. Mike had gotten a $30 check for his medical expenses. Savages came out to the house and offered to give him the $30 to help pay for the car. Savages had just added insult to injury. Dad used some words I hadn't ever heard him use and told them they better get out of his house. Now the old '56 Chevy lives with the old '49 truck down in the draw behind my house.

Chapter 24
Building Our House

On September 19, 1961, Keith was born. The next spring, Dad said it looked like I was going to stick with farming and he wanted to build a house for us on his farm west of Verdella. Willy Bowman had helped build their house so Dad asked if he would help on this house. We went into Liberal and looked at the Bowman's house. It looked just like what we wanted.

Tom, Wilma & Keith Alan Crockett

Wilma's dad and her Uncle Dean laid the foundation. We paid Willy and his partner, Mr. Foster $1.50 an hour and Herb Waring $1.25 an hour. The carpenters were there thirty days and the total labor bill was $1,000. Mom and Wilma did all the finish work. Dad and I did all the electric, heating and plumbing. Grandma Bunton did the babysitting. We started the house in September and moved in before Christmas.

Four Generations at Emmet & Jessie Bunton's 50th Anniversary
Tom Crockett, Marjorie Bunton Crockett, Keith Crockett
Emmet & Jessie Bunton

To get a little more income, we started raising pigs. Everett had the sows and baby pigs at his place. Then we brought the little pigs to our place to fatten them up. The hogs made up a big part of our income.

Grandpa Bunton had retired and put his whole farm in the Soil Bank and sowed fescue on it. After it came out of the Soil Bank, we put an electric fence around the whole farm. We would drive all the cattle from Dad's place to Grandpa's in the fall. This was all on foot and with horses. When we drove them down Highway 43, some people didn't appreciate cattle in the road and would go to honking and scatter cows and calves in every direction.

After a year or two the cows knew what was going on, so they didn't need too much herding. On the other hand, the calves would get behind so that was where the work was.

I thought that we should have another baby. Wilma said there is too much pain involved and she didn't want to go through that again. I kept on until she said yes. On June 1st, 1965, our daughter was born. Wilma said after Michelle was born that we had a boy and a girl so we had all the kids we needed. The proudest days of my life were when our two babies were born. There were times during her labor that she wished she could kill me so I see why she thought two was enough.

Wilma, Keith, Tom & Michelle Lynn Crockett

Chapter 25

John Deere Machinery
(and the Purinton Hunting Trip)

In 1963, we had started farming some of Grandpa Bunton's ground. Martin Foger, who had 320 acres just east of Grandpa had arthritis so bad he could no longer farm. Martin asked us if we would like to rent his farm. I told Dad we better take him up on that. That meant we needed a bigger tractor. Dad traded our Allis WD for a D19 Allis propane. I didn't like it much better than our WD. The seat was in the middle right above the transmission which was hot. Then you were behind the odorous propane tank with fumes right in your face. If it was below 40 degrees, it wouldn't start.

Happy Curless was the Allis dealer in Liberal. We kept taking it back to see if they could fix it. Never was any better but one day, Hap called up and said that they had figured something out. Could we bring it in? We took it to town and left it. A few days later Hap called up and said they had it fixed. I went in to get it and it wouldn't start.

Happy was embarrassed but he put a chain on and pulled it. I left the key off so of course, it wouldn't start. I made him pull me down Main Street before I turned the key back on. Maybe a dirty trick, but I'd about had it with it not starting.

Every fall when I was plowing, third gear would go out. (I actually got to move up to third gear by this time.) I think Allis had put a bigger motor on a WD transmission.

We had enough of our D19. Dad decided to trade it for a 4020 John Deere. Happy wasn't very happy about that.

Jack Purinton was the John Deere Dealer in Lamar. Dad liked to talk with him about the old days when Dad had the grocery store in Irwin and Jack had a truck route delivering ice. He would tell Dad that he was still selling the 50# ice block on Friday that he had purchased on Monday. Then Dad would come back that it was bad enough that Jack was selling 50# ice that he'd started with in the morning by that evening.

After negotiating the price of trading one afternoon, Dad stopped by my place and said that Jack had been out in Wyoming elk hunting when Guy Ross, another guy who was hunting with them, had a heart attack. Jack had flown back to Lamar with Guy. Jack's other buddy, Art Stoltz, had stayed out there. They had made a camper out of an old school bus and used it to pull a jeep out there. Jack said he needed someone to go back to Wyoming with him. He had a new Chevy that he was going to drive to Wyoming to finish up his elk hunt and then would pull the jeep home with his pickup. He was needing someone to drive the bus back home.

Non-residents had to have a guide for hunting. They knew some people who had moved to Wyoming from Lamar. Charles Dockery, his son-in-law Frank Rush and grandson Duane would qualify as guides since they lived in Wyoming.

I told Dad it sounded like fun and I would love to go. Sam Foster, who was working in the John Deere shop, also volunteered to go. Jack said after they finished their elk hunt, Frank & Duane would take Sam and me deer hunting.

I didn't have a deer rifle so I went to Pittsburg. I had earlier bought a shotgun from a guy called Cactus Jack. He said he would loan me a 7mm German Mauser.

Jack, Sam and I left Lamar at 6 a.m. When we got to I-70 the speed limit was 80 mph so we put the pickup on 90 mph. We would trade off driving and that night we got a motel room in Casper, Wyoming.

The campground where the bus was at was just below Yellowstone Park. This was the first of November. The way the elk hunt was supposed to go was like this: When a big snowstorm hits in the park, the elk migrate south to Jackson Hole where there is a big refuge. They would spend the winter there.

It was snowing when we got to camp so things were looking good in the morning. We would drive up to the border of the park and harvest elk as they come out. We spent the day up there and never saw any elk.

The next day they decided to hunt locally. That next morning Art, Frank, Duane, Jack, and I headed up a mountain about five miles from camp. Frank had a pony, about the size of my old pony Betsy, that he rode every day. We walked up an old logging road and then would fan out and walk back down through the timber. We would see elk tracks going down and then we'd go by a ten-acre meadow. Same thing happened three mornings in a row.

That night Art, Jack and I went down to Jackson to buy groceries. We decided to eat while we were in town. At a table next to us was a couple of men. One of them said he wanted to shoot his guide because the guide had let him shoot a moose that was standing in five feet of water. Made it impossible to get it out.

That gave me the idea of being a guide. I told Jack the elk had done the same thing three days in a row. I said, "Why don't you three guys with guns set up by that meadow and Duane and I will go up like always. Maybe that elk will come out and one of you can get a shot."

That sounded good to them. The next morning, we all did as I had suggested. As Duane and I were walking up, I hit Duane in the chest. "What?" he asked.

There was an elk walking down that same road. We froze. That elk wasn't twenty yards from us. Duane had already shot an elk and I didn't have a permit so neither one of us had a gun. The elk took off the wrong direction and my heart sank. If we'd all be walking up as we had before, someone could have had an elk. We should have had at least one man with a gun. But we continued on with my plan.

When we got to the meadow, there was Jack with an elk had done just what I had predicted. Jack had a 300-yard shot and got the elk with one shot. Jack had the head mounted and it hung in his John Deere store until the store sold a couple of years ago.

The next day, Jack and Art loaded up the jeep and headed home. Sam and I followed Duane to his house in Thermopolis, Wyoming.

The following day, Sam and I got our deer tags and rode with Duane about fifty miles to his cousin's ranch. Frank followed with his pony. Frank told Sam and I where we should go and he would ride around the base of this little mountain and try to drive the deer to us.

As I was walking up a gully, a monster buck jumped up. I was close. I fired my first shot. He kept on walking. I shot again. Still walking. With my last shot he had gotten to the top of the hill. He turned around and stood there. I missed again.

That stupid Mauser had peep sights and I couldn't get a good bead on him. Now I see why the Germans lost the war.

I went on to the top where I had last seen the deer. There was blood. I had hit him. Frank saw me and rode up and said he had followed the blood until the deer had stopped bleeding then couldn't find a trace of the deer.

While we were talking Frank said, "There is a buck and four doe!"

There again I couldn't get a good bead on the buck. When I shot, Frank said, "You gut shot him." Great. Let's stay here and see if he will lay down. The buck did lay down so we went down where I could get close, and I would be able to get a clean shot. Finally, I got my first deer. Sam had gotten a little one. Now we could start home in the old bus.

The next morning, we loaded our deer in the back of the bus. We went to fill up with gas and the differential was making some noise. Thought we better check. It hardly had any oil in it. It was a good thing we checked. We didn't pass up very many truck stops to put oil in the differential.

We drove all day. Sam and I would trade off driving so we didn't stop unless we needed oil...which became more and more often. Sometime that night we stopped at a truck stop on I-70 and there was a boy hitchhiking. He said he was headed to Michigan and wanted to know if he could ride with us. I said, "I don't know. I'll ask Sam."

Sam said, "We are the ones with guns so it will probably be okay."

He rode with us all night. That morning we stopped to fill up with gas and oil and to eat breakfast. We all ordered but before the boy had finished eating, he got up and went out to the bus. The waitress said, "That boy didn't pay."

"I'll take care of it," I said.

When I got back, the boy was getting his things off the bus. I told him that I would have bought his meal but since he tried to sneak out, he could start walking.

We drove all day again. By the time we got to Lawrence, Kansas that differential was screaming. We made it home about dark. Sam let me off at home and he went on to Lamar.

That was the last trip that bus ever made.

74

Chapter 26

Water Skiing

I finally found a sport I could excel at. That was water skiing. Although the first time I went water skiing, it almost turned into a tragedy.

Don Bainter said he had been talking to Clarence Ihms about renting a boat from him. Clarence showed him a real nice boat that he could rent and take to Grand Lake. Don said he, Jim Bainter and Jim Hanshaw were going. Don said, "Why don't you come along and we will teach you how to ski."

Sounded like fun so I said, "Sure."

When we went to pick up the boat, it wasn't the same boat. Clarence said he had sold the boat Don had looked at. The boat he wanted us to use was older and had a lot smaller motor. But Don said, "Okay, I guess we will take it."

This was in May right after school was out. The water was still pretty cold and I couldn't get up on skis with that small motor.

Don and Jim Bainter both already knew how to ski so they took turns. Jim Bainter was driving pulling Don. Jim Hanshaw was cold and sitting in the back of the boat all hunkered down. We were all watching Don when I looked up and saw something in the water right in front of the boat. I yelled, "Watch out!"

Jim Bainter whipped the boat throwing Jim Hanshaw out into the lake. Jim hollered, "He can't swim!" Hanshaw had all his clothes, shoes, and Ag jacket on. When I looked back, he was fighting the water with all he had.

It took us a little while to turn the boat around and get back to Jim. Don dropped off his skis and got to Jim first. Hanshaw was still panicking pounding on Don.

We got back and pulled up beside them. With Don pushing and Jim Bainter pulling we got Hanshaw back in the boat. He just laid there. We didn't know if he was still alive or not.

Finally, he started moving so we knew he was still alive. Patricks who used to live in Liberal had a resort nearby, so we took Hanshaw up there to get him dried off and dressed in some dry clothes.

That was the end of our ski trip and thank the Lord it didn't end in Hanshaw drowning. Maybe everyone should have had a life jacket on.

A few years later, Wilma's Uncle Dean invited us to go skiing with him. Dean and Harold's cousins owned a strip pit three miles north of Frontenac that was shaped in a circle. Dean had a nice boat with a bigger motor than the boat we rented from Ihms. After a few tries, I got up and was hooked on water skiing.

Not too long after that Harold bought a boat. There was a pit that was ½ mile long two miles north of Frontenac that we would go to every Sunday afternoon. I would bring the gas and we went through 15 or 20 gallons every time. If everything went right you could make it around the south end but would have to start over on the north end.

It wasn't long before I would kick off one ski and ski on one. Then I learned how to drag one foot until I got up. I never used two skis again.

Don Bainter bought a boat, and we met him and Shirley up at Lake Pomme De Terre one weekend. His boat was big enough to get Don and me up on single skis. Everything was going great. I was over on the left side of the wake. Don was going back and forth jumping the wakes. Don made a sharp left turn and jumped the wake next to me. When he jumped that wake, he went airborne, couldn't turn, and ran over me. I didn't know he was coming until SMACK! It took a year for my right shoulder not to hurt. Can you hear the bomb ticking?

Falling off Cyclone and being run over by Don were a couple of things that meant that shoulder would have to be replaced.

Chapter 27

A Boat of Our Own

One Sunday we were at Wilma's folks when Bob Crockett called and said that his neighbor had a boat for sale. The neighbor's wife was going to have a baby and he had to sell the boat. Bob lived in Frontenac at that time so we went right over and looked at it. It was a Johnson boat and trailer about five years old. It looked very nice so we took it over to Farlington Lake north of Girard to check it out. We fell in love with that boat so we helped Bob's neighbor out and bought it.

Wilma driving with Louise as spotter

Stockton Lake was new and had filled up. It was just 45 miles east of us so we could get there in less than an hour. Most Sunday afternoons would find us over at Hawker Point on Lake Stockton if the weather would let us. Wilma was able to ski two or three times a day and never get her hair wet so if we got home in time, we could still go to church.

In the summer of 1978, we started camping with Mike and Kathy, and Denny and Louise and their boys at the State Park on Table Rock Lake. We would meet every summer in August until Mike and Kathy moved to Bryan, Texas. When they moved to Denton, Texas we all started meeting there again. This time it was in Condos instead of camping.

One afternoon in 2001, we took all the grandkids over to Stockton and taught them how to ski. It took most of the day but they all skied a little. I told Chad that if he would drive the boat, I would ski a little. I didn't see a jacket so I put on a belt. Keith had a single ski that was too narrow for my foot but I got it on. I was dragging a foot as usual. After pulling me for a little bit without a jacket, I could see that I wasn't going to get up. I let loose of the rope. My foot didn't come out of the ski and I felt a tremendous pain. I tore my hamstring on my right leg. That ended my skiing career. I tried a few times after that, but I never could get up.

Chapter 28

Sadder Times

Up to this point in writing this little book, I have relived some adventures, some close calls, and some funny/some stupid things. Now comes a hard part that's hard to relive. I don't know the best way to put down the words.

One day I went up to Everett's and Dad was sitting down in a lot of pain.

"What can I do?" I asked.

Dad said he would be okay; he just needed to rest a little bit. The pain did go away after a while.

Not too long after that, it happened again. That's when he decided to go to a heart doctor. Dad was told he had Angina (constricting pain below the sternum, most easily precipitated by exertion or excitement.) He needed to lose some weight. He cut down on what he ate and weight came off quickly.

Of a morning Dad couldn't walk slow enough because the pain was real bad. By afternoon he could haul hay.

I was helping him haul and he said, "I think I'm in better shape than you are." I wish that had been the case.

In July of 1969, we lost our Grandad Barney. He'd always been really special to us grandkids and it was something I think we all took really hard. It was the first death in the family for us. We were glad he and Grandma had already moved from Irwin to their Senior Citizen apartment in Lamar so it wasn't as hard for her as it would have been to have the sale and move after he had passed.

That summer we had bought a grain bin from Donnie Thomas. Getting milo dry after harvesting it that August was quite a chore. Dad thought that this bin would dry it down enough overnight and then we could move it to the barn where it would stay until we sold it. The first load we put in the bin was about 1500 bushel running 19% moisture. Dad turned the propane burner on that evening.

The next morning it hadn't dried any. Dad talked to Donnie and he said we hadn't turned the heat up enough. That night Dad turned the heat up to where Donnie said to put it.

The following morning, I was pulling into Everett's when I saw Dad putting a ladder up on the bin. "What's wrong?" I yelled.

"The bin is on fire!"

"Should I go call the fire department?"

"Yes!"

I ran into Everett's house and told them what was going on. When I came out, Dad was walking up to the house when he collapsed in the driveway.

Everett and I did everything we could think of. I was giving mouth to mouth resuscitation and Everett was working on his chest. Neither one of us knew much about trying to help in this situation. I knew time wasn't on our side and it wasn't long before he went to be with the Lord.

I've always believed that our time here on earth is written down and when it's our time, nothing is going to change it.

That afternoon I went back over to Everett's to see if the Firemen had gotten the fire out. They had and there hadn't been much damage done to the bin. Some of the milo was charcoal, but it wasn't hurt much.

With the next batch of milo, I set the bin on fire. We finally figured out that we had used cement blocks under the floor and the flame would hit them and then shoot up towards the milo. We fixed it by turning the blocks sideways so the hot air would go over the whole bin.

Chapter 29

Crockett Farms, Inc.

On the afternoon the day Dad died, Everett came out of his house and said, "I want you to run things like your Dad did."

I went from being Number 3 to running the farm. Dad had made all the decisions. Now I was going to have to do that.

That evening we all went back over to Mom's house. Uncle Ray, Uncle Paul and Uncle Don were all there. I told them what Everett wanted to do. They said that they were confident I could make it work. I didn't have much of a choice but to try.

I talked to Jim McClendon about how Everett and I should handle our business. Jim suggested that we should incorporate. He set up an appointment with an attorney in Joplin for us. We set up Crockett Farms, Inc. I bought Dad's half of the machinery and we put all the machinery in the corporation. We kept all our own land and rented it to the corporation. That way Crockett Farms was the boss. We made it work until Everett retired.

In 1974 Max Kentner, Pete Minor's son-in-law pulled in at Everett's and said they were ready to sell Pete's farm. We had been renting the farm for twenty-some years. Max said that they wanted $800 an acre and that they would carry the note.

I said, "Yes, I'd like to buy it."

The next morning, Everett said that he wanted to sell his farm and his half of the machinery. WOW. Here we go again. How am I going to pull this off?

Keith had decided to farm with us when he got out of high school. The government had some low interest loans for young people wanting to get into farming. I told Keith he should get one of those loans and buy Everett's farm and half of his half of the machinery. I would buy Minor's land and the other half of Everett's machinery. That's how we pulled it off.

One night three or four years later, we were cutting beans down south. It was real muddy and we were having a hard time. We were on the west side of the draw when Keith called up and said that he was stuck and the N7 Gleaner was sitting on its frame with all four wheels spinning in mud.

On our way home that night Keith said that the day he said he wanted to farm was the stupidest day of his life. That wasn't the last time for those thoughts.

Chapter 30
The Boys Who Worked for Us

After Everett and I started farming together, we knew we would need help in the summer. To fill the gap, we hired neighbor boys. Our first was Lynn Hoover, then his brother, Craig. They lived just a mile from Everett's so they could work after school as well.

Next was Kurt Holland. One day we were working up at Bronaugh. It had been real wet and we were way late planting our soybeans. We were waiting for the ground to dry a little more. Kurt was caught up and didn't have anything to do. I needed to spray some more and the sprayer tank was empty. In Bronaugh there was a place by the city well where I could fill up quickly and it only cost fifty cents for 500 gallons.

I told Kurt to go to town and fill the tank. I gave him two quarters, then I said, "In case it doesn't fill it, here is another quarter."

He was gone a long time. I knew it shouldn't take that long. Finally, he came back with only about 25 gallons in the sprayer. He said that seventy-five cents didn't put but five gallons in it so he went to the grocery store and borrowed $5. That didn't get very much more so he went back and tried to borrow $20 more. They wouldn't give it to him so that is why the tank only had 25 gallons in it.

What I didn't know is that he went to the car wash. I didn't even know there was a car wash and he didn't know you could buy water at the well.

Kurt asked me, "Are you going to pay the $5 I borrowed at the grocery store?"

"No! I told you that fifty cents would fill it. You were the Valedictorian of your class and you couldn't figure out that there was something wrong before you borrowed $5?"

I had a good laugh and then went to the store and paid the $5. Glad they hadn't given him another $20 in quarters.

After Everett retired, Keith and I still needed help. These are some of the boys that worked for us: Dean Buffington, Eric "Okey Doke" Yount, Mike Warner, Brent Hanshaw and Brent Fast. Brent started when he was thirteen years old and helped until he started college. By that time, Chad took over working and is still with Keith and me.

All the boys were great workers and I thank them all.

Chapter 31
Wilma's Dad

When we moved to Verdella, the draw behind our house was full of quail. For those of you who don't know, quail are small birds that live in coveys on the ground. They have nearly disappeared today. There are many reasons: lack of ground cover, more predators like hawks, coyotes, bobcats, raccoons, and wild turkeys just to name a few.

Harold, Wilma's dad, saw all the quail we had here and bought a new shotgun and a bird dog. It was a pointer he named Vick. Harold could hunt all day behind our house and get his limit, usually eight or ten birds. He said I should get a shotgun and hunt with him. I went over to Pittsburg and bought a Model 12 Winchester from Cactus Jack.

After I started hunting with him, we needed another dog. I bought an Irish setter named Pat. She was okay but not as good as Vick. About every weekend during quail season, we went hunting.

When Harold was in his 40's he had a couple of heart attacks. Wilma's mother Rosie worried about him hunting. I told her I didn't know about his heart but there was nothing wrong with his legs. He could out walk me.

One Sunday afternoon in 1975 we were hunting north of Verdella on Lee Bunton's farm. We were hunting down a hedge row when Vick walked by a quail. Vick didn't see or smell it. Harold said, "What's the matter with you, Vick?" Just then Vick fell over dead. Vick had made his last hunt.

A few days later, I had gone over to Lockwood to see about trading combines. When I got home Wilma said her dad had come out to hunt with the Irish setter bird dog he had gotten a few years earlier. She said, "Dad waited a while for you but decided to go on alone."

That night Rosie called up and said that Harold hadn't come home. That didn't sound good so we told her that Keith and I would go look. I knew all the places he liked to hunt. One of his favorites was starting at Grandpa Bunton's then going down Martin Foger's hedge row.

When Keith and I turned into Grandpa Bunton's driveway, I noticed that the gate was fastened on the inside. That meant that Harold had been up that way. Harold's pickup was sitting at the end of the driveway so I got on the CB and told Wilma we had found his truck. Back then everybody had CBs so before long there were dozens helping in the search.

Keith and I followed our usual trail. When we got down to the south end of the hedgerow and we started back up the east side. We didn't go far until Harold's bird dog let out a yell.

We found Harold. He still had his shotgun in his hands and had fallen face first. I was glad that Keith and I were the ones to find him. It wasn't long before other people arrived. Max Rose was one of the guys. Max looked in Harold's coat and said there were five quail in it.

It was really hard to go back home and tell Wilma, her mother and sisters that we had found Harold and that he was gone. Any other time I would have been with him but there wouldn't have been anything I could have done.

That ended my quail hunting. I don't think I ever went again.

Chapter 32

Scares We've Had

The kids had a couple of close calls too. First when Michelle was around eleven, she'd gotten a new Beta fish and fishbowl. I had come home from work and was getting ready to take a shower. I'd just taken my shirt off when I heard a scream from Michelle's bedroom. We went running in there. She had filled the fishbowl and was carrying it back to her room when the bowl broke in half. One of the pieces of glass cut deeply into her right wrist. I put my thumb in the cut to stop the bleeding.

Wilma drove and we went to the emergency room at Nevada Hospital. The Emergency Room was full, so we had to wait for our turn. I kept my thumb on the cut the whole time. It seemed to take forever. We finally got a doctor to look at it. After examining her he said the nerves had been cut and we needed to take her to Kansas City. We needed a Specialist to try to make the repair.

The doctor in Nevada put in some stitches and off to KC we went. I had a CB radio in the car and when we got to town I got on and asked for help getting to the hospital. A guy came back and asked where we were at. I told him what street we were on at a stop light. He said he was at the same light and to follow him.

When we got to the hospital, I thanked him and rushed Michelle into the hospital. The Nevada hospital had called and told them the situation and they had a doctor ready.

While Michelle was in the Operating Room, I called Denny and asked if he could bring me a shirt. He and Louise came to be with us. When the doctor came out, he said that nerves are not color coded and he did the best he could. He said if they weren't in exactly the right place her hand would be clawed. We did a lot of praying.

After it had healed, we took her back. When the doctor took off the bandage he said, "It's a miracle or I'm good." I think he had a little help during the operation. Her hand isn't perfect but close.

In 2012, Keith bought a horse for his girlfriend. One day in December, Keith and I were doing some business in Lamar. Keith said, "When we get home, I think I'll saddle up and go for a ride."

I had gone to Bronaugh to put a bull into a different pasture when Wilma called and said, "Something bad has happened to Keith and I think he has had a heart attack!"

I got there as fast as the old blue pickup could go. When I got there, Wilma said, "I made him take seven aspirins."

I said, "He didn't have a heart attack. I think that horse reared up and fell backwards on him." Wilma didn't know about the horse. I told her, "The horse is standing in the pasture with a saddle hanging upside down, so I think that's how he got hurt."

Keith had his phone and had been able to call his mom and tell her he was lying in the driveway but didn't know how he got there and he couldn't move.

Wilma said when her dad had his heart attack the doctor said to give him seven aspirins and that was why Keith got seven aspirins.

When the paramedics arrived and started cutting Keith's shirt off, he was screaming. I guess I went into shock. I don't remember anything until we got to Freeman Hospital. The paramedics had a helicopter to take Keith and we got there about the same time.

I went into the ER to see him and he said, "Boy, I have heartburn."

I said, "Yes, you do. I think the seven aspirins did it."

He had a broken tendon in his shoulder, most of his ribs were either broken or cracked. They operated and put some pins in the ribs and a cadaver tendon in the shoulder.

Everything worked out and the Lord was looking out for him. His time bomb almost went off.

Chapter 33

One More Miracle

After Michelle retired from her career as a secretary for the Liberal School District, she began coming down to help cook dinner. That was our main meal of the day and Keith, Chad and sometimes Sara and Cooper would come to our house at noon. In the middle of June 2023, Michelle told us she was having some sharp chest pains. They didn't last long but she'd had them a couple of other times. She made an appointment with my heart specialist, Dr. Ko, for Friday, June 23.

On Thursday she said she wasn't going to do anything that might set it off. When I got home that afternoon, I noticed a 50# sack of sunflower seeds on the inside of our fence. When asked, she said was at Orchslan's going out of business sale and couldn't pass up the deal she was able to get. She bought one bag for us and one for herself. Of course, that meant loading and unloading those bags herself.

The next morning, we had a call from Michelle at 6:30 saying she'd had a heart attack the night before and was in a room at Mercy Hospital in Joplin. About 10:30 the night before it felt like someone had put an axe in her back. Doug raced her to the hospital. Ironically, Dr. Ko was the one on call and would be taking care of her. At the very time she was supposed to be in his office for a new patient appointment, he was in the operating room with her.

When he did the scope, he found her widow-maker artery was 90% plugged. After he put a stent in, she felt better immediately. None of the other arteries had any sign of blockage. She was able to come home that same day.

On the way to Joplin, Michelle thought her time bomb was ticking very fast. Thank the Lord, He watches over us.

Chapter 34
Farm Bureau

In the Spring of 1970, Wilma and I were chosen to serve on the Farm Bureau Young Farmer committee for Barton County. That summer we were invited to go to Excelsior Springs to the State Young Farmer Convention. There we met couples from all over the state.

The next Spring, we were asked to serve on the State Young Farmer committee for a two-year term. We made a lot of good friends and still stay in touch with some of them to this day.

In our second year we got a list of new couples that would serve. Most of our meetings were in Jefferson City. I noticed one of the couples was from Halfway which was close to us. I called and asked if they would like to ride with us. We picked them up on our way to Jefferson City and we became the best of friends with Ken and Becky Legan.

When we went over to their house, Michelle would get car sick. Years later when Chad had a basketball game in Boliver, Michelle rode with us to the game. She said she remembered every place we had to stop to let her throw up.

Jim and Dorothy Keopke from Bourbon, Floyd and Joan Massa from Lebanon, and Larry and Betty Newhem from Norborn are the other couples that we have stayed in touch with.

Chapter 35

Pioneer Seed

The Lord works in mysterious ways sometimes.

In the Fall of 1974, it was wet and we were having a hard time cutting our soybeans. It was the day after Thanksgiving and our John Deere 4400 combine broke down. I went to Lamar to get parts. It was a shock, but they didn't have the piece that I needed.

Paul Ricketts also had a 4400 combine and he was also broken down. When I told them what I needed, Paul said that his parts wouldn't be in for a few days and I could go take the part I needed off his combine. Then I could put my new part back on his combine when it came in. I went and found his combine and got what I needed.

The next Spring, I decided to plant some Pioneer milo. At that time Paul sold Pioneer seed so I went to Bronaugh and bought a few bags of seed from him.

One day a horn honked and a woman came to the door. Wilma answered it but she didn't know the woman. The woman said, "I'm Blanche Ricketts and I would like Tom to farm my land. My husband Paul passed away and I need to rent my farm. Have Tom come up and I will show him the land."

I went up and we drove around to look it over. She said she wanted cash rent and I would also have to rent the farm that they had been renting from Russell Horn. Horn's farm was right next to their land and she wanted it to stay together.

Blanche said that she and Paul had driven by our place and Paul had said that if he ever rented out his farm, he would like Tom Crockett to farm it. She also said that she couldn't rent to any one of her neighbors because whichever one she picked would make the other neighbors mad. She also said that I could have the Pioneer dealership.

Rickett's farm was 450 acres and Horn's was 310 acres. I told her, "I have to talk to Everett and Wilma. This is about double what we are doing now."

Everett said it was up to me. "Remember, I told you that you were the boss."

I said, "We are going to need fulltime help or get bigger machinery."

Craig Hoover helped a couple of years and Keith was old enough to do a lot of work. Blanche passed away in 1995 and Keith and I bought her place from her daughter Pat in 1996.

Russell Horn lived in Lebanon, Ohio. I called and rented his farm over the phone. One day I was going by our house on a tractor and saw a man knocking on our door. I thought he was just a salesman but noticed he was driving a BMW so thought maybe I better stop.

As I walked up he said, "You don't know me, do you?"

"No, I'm sorry. I don't"

"I'm Russell Horn."

I'm glad I stopped. You should be nice to your landlord. We rented his farm until he and his wife passed away. Then we bought Horn's farm in 2016.

When I rented Blanche Rickett's farm in 1977, I got the Pioneer dealership. George Born was my boss and became a good friend. When I started, milo was the seed I sold the most. Dry land corn was pretty risky and the only corn I sold was to people who irrigated. Pioneer wasn't into soybeans or wheat so $25 per bag milo didn't generate much commission.

In the 90's dry land corn became more dependable and milo sales started to decline until everyone switched to corn and my milo sales went to zero. Back in the 60's Pete Minor wanted to see a 100-bushel yield on corn but he didn't live to see it. In 2021 we had the perfect corn year. We had some corn make 230-bushel dry land.

When I started selling, Dave Garst had Missouri and part of Iowa as a sales area for Pioneer. A few years later Pioneer and Garst had a falling out and went their separate ways. The next year all we had to sell was leftover Pioneer seed and new Garst seed.

Garst seed didn't do very well so it looked like my seed business was over. I heard that Pioneer had gotten into soybean seed and I had a chance to sell it if I wanted to.

I called Pioneer and asked if I could start selling beans. They said yes, so I was back with Pioneer. The next year we got both corn and milo to sell and Pioneer also started selling soft wheat seed. George Born got his old job back and he was my boss again.

Pioneer came out with a new program of deferred payment. You could defer pay your seed in the fall of one year and not have to pay the balance until the next December. You got the early pay discounts and interest was 1% below prime.

Farmers thought it was a great idea but Wall Street didn't. Pioneer stock went to pot and DuPont bought them out. Things changed again and DuPont didn't want small farmer dealers. They wanted large dealers that only sold Pioneer seed full-time.

George retired and Jerry Marley took his place. Jerry's job was to get rid of the small dealers and get one person that would take over. Jerry asked me to resign, and I said, "No, I won't resign. You will have to fire me."

Jerry said that he couldn't fire anyone that year but he would the next. I talked to Jerry's boss and told him I really wanted to stay. They talked it over. I could stay but I was on a very short leash. Mike and Matt Bunton were the dealers to the East of me. Mike told Jerry they would quit and give me their territory. That way I would have a bigger area. Jerry agreed to that so I started selling in the Irwin area.

I got an email saying that Pioneer was looking for a guy who would intern with them for the summer. His job would be to work with dealers over the western half of Missouri. I told Chad about the job and he got it.

After that summer Pioneer said that I could have Chad as an associate. Since Chad had worked for Pioneer, they let him take over my dealership. After forty years I let Chad take over fulltime.

P.S. I outlasted Jerry Marley.

Chapter 36

NASCAR

When Doug worked at O'Sullivan's, some of his friends got him interested in car racing. O'Sullivan's sponsored a race car. We went to Bolivar a few times to watch it. There was a kid from Joplin who raced in the same class as the O'Sullivan car. It was said he was good enough to drive a cup car someday. That kid did make it to the Big Time. His name is Jamie McMurry. McMurry is now retired, but he did win some big races in his career.

In the summer of 1996, Wilma and I were looking for some place to get away for a few days. Michelle and Doug asked, "Why don't you go to Bristol, Tennessee to the NASCAR race? It's a night-time short track race with a lot of action."

It was too late to order tickets, but you can always find someone scalping tickets. Tried to find a motel, but the closest vacancy was in Knoxville, Tennessee, ninety miles away. We decided okay, we'll stay there the first night then drive to Bristol the next day.

We were able to buy a couple of scalp tickets and go to the race. It was a rainy day. The race got delayed and didn't get over until midnight. We found a V Highway shortcut road that would get us from the racetrack to the main highway. Lots of cars were leaving the track so it took a long time to get on the road back to Knoxville.

I missed the shortcut but figured the road we were on was going in the right direction so we would eventually find a road to get back on the four lane. After a while, something didn't seem right. You know a Crockett never gets turned around or lost, right? Finally saw a sign and we were in North Carolina. We'd never get to Knoxville this way. We backtracked to Bristol, found the right road and got to Knoxville at 4 a.m.

The next day we drove to Gatlinburg and spent three days driving in the Smoky Mountains. We were eating at a Cracker Barrel one night. When we got back in the pickup, it sounded like something fell out. We looked but didn't find anything.

On our way home, I slammed on the brakes and came to a screeching halt. I had known we would be driving at night on strange roads so I had put my pistol under the seat of the pickup. That noise must have been the pistol falling out of the truck! What if someone found it and robbed a bank or shot someone? In a panic, I looked under the seat. The gun was still there. Thank the Lord! Never did know just what we heard back there at the Cracker Barrel parking lot.

The next year we were again wondering where to go on a trip. We got to talking to the kids and told them we had fun at Bristol, why don't we all go?

Once again, we couldn't find a motel in Bristol but found one at Pigeon Forge, a little closer than Knoxville. Pigeon Forge is a lot like Branson with shows and a lot of things for kids to do, and I knew how to get to the racetrack using the shortcut. There were scalpers selling tickets the year before so we could buy our tickets once we got there.

When we got to the shortcut road it was closed so we had to go back to Bristol to get to the racetrack. We drove quite a few miles and wound up in Bristol, Virginia! Heading back to the racetrack we saw plenty of people selling tickets. At a filling station there were some guys with a sign. We pulled in and parked around back. A man asked if we needed tickets. Yes, we did so we followed him to his car where he opened the trunk. The tickets weren't double in price but close.

About that time, cops were arresting the guys out front. The guy we were dealing with slammed his trunk and went squalling down the street. Did we get scalped? What if the tickets were fake?? We wouldn't know until we tried to get in at the racetrack. The tickets were good so we did get to see the race.

The next year a new track opened in Texas about fifteen miles south of Denton. We got online and found tickets, but the seats were on the back stretch. The closest motel room was in McKinney, thirty miles east of Denton.

When we checked in the lady asked what time we wanted a wake-up call. The race didn't start until noon so we didn't think we needed to get up early. She said, "Why, everyone else is getting up at 5 a.m. because it has rained so much, the grass parking area has turned into a mud lot."

Okay. We got up at 5:00 and went. When we got about five miles from the track, I-35W was a parking lot. It took forever to get in and finding a place to park was a nightmare. Finally got parked and had to walk a long way to get to our seats.

When we left, I took a side road that went by a ranch next to the track. There was a long lane up to the house and I thought maybe we could pay them and park there the next day. The lady said yes, we could park there for $10. That sounded good so we parked there the next day. We had to walk a little further but getting out would be much easier.

We each had different drivers we were rooting for. Kiley's driver was Terry Labonte. She was yelling for Terry when the guy sitting next to her said, "You know I am a Labonte?"

Kiley said, "You know I'm a Kiley?"

He said the Labonte brothers were his cousins.

When we got back to our car, the couple that lived there were sitting on the porch drinking lemonade. The lady said, "If Daddy could see that racetrack across the road he would be turning over in his grave." I could see the dollar signs in her husband's eyes though.

Sometimes when I'm watching a Texas Motor Speedway race on tv, the camera scans around the area. It's easy to see that property is no longer a ranch. I think they probably did very well.

Chapter 37

Other Trips We've Enjoyed

In 1976, Farm Bureau had the national convention in Hawaii. Ken and Becky, Jim and Dorothy, and Wilma and I all made the trip. We thought about attending some of the convention but renting a van and touring the island sounded like more fun. There were five couples crammed into the van, but we had a ball. The van was a piece of junk. It burned more oil than gas and smoked like a steam engine. No problem when you are having fun.

Wilma and I were invited to Ken and Becky's daughter's wedding in 2000. While we were there, Ken asked us if we would like to drive to Alaska the next summer. I jumped on that and said sure. We left here in July and got back in August. Becky kept a daily journal so if you want to read about that the trip I have a copy. You can find out what we ate, how much it cost, where we stayed at night. Everything you might want to know (or not!)

Wilma & Tom in Alaska

In 2004, Chad got invited to play football on a team from Kansas. The games were played in Hawaii so John and Judy Rawlings and Wilma and I went to watch him play. The team did very well and won all their games.

While we were there, we went to Pearl Harbor. We saw the Arizona where it still rests on the bottom of the harbor. That day happened to be the 60th anniversary of the signing of the surrender of WWII with Japan on the battleship Missouri. We were late for the official ceremony. When we told them we were from Lamar, Missouri, the town where Harry Truman was born, we got a special guided tour. We got to see the place where President Truman and the Emperor of Japan did the signing.

In 2010, Wilma and I would be celebrating our 50th anniversary. We wanted to do something special, so we took our whole family to Maui for a week. There were seventeen of us. Everyone had a good time except Sadie. She was only two and didn't like the airplane ride. She cried from LA to Maui. I know everyone on that plane enjoyed the trip. She wanted to lay down in the aisle, but we were in the back of the plane next to the restrooms. Too much traffic.

After our wonderful plane ride, we went to get the two vans I had rented. After filling out the paperwork and showing my driver's license and credit card, we drove across the island to Lahaina where our condo was. The manager asked to see my credit card and driver's license. They weren't in my billfold! I figured I must have left them at the rental company. I called, but no they didn't see them anywhere there.

It had been a long day. Everyone was tired and we couldn't check into our rooms. It was going to be a long trip with no credit card or driver's license. Keith said we could use his so we could at least get to bed.

After we got in our room, I took out my billfold and looked in every compartment. Sure enough, I put them in a place I'd never put them before. It was where I kept my fishing license, social security card and things like that. When I'd look in a hurry they were covered up and I completely overlooked them. Kiley has never let me forget that.

I rented a big boat for all the men to go deep sea fishing. It turned into a deep-sea boat ride. No fish.

One side trip was to Haleakala to the rim of a dormant volcano. It is dotted with great cinder cones in varied colors. One other trip was to Hana which has a black sand beach. From there we went to the 45-foot Waimea Falls and a natural swimming pool. Some of the kids jumped off a cliff into the pool. I watched from a safe distance.

Chapter 38

D.C. Trip

In 1998, we took a trip to Washington, D.C. We stayed with friends Russell and Phyllis Detridge who lived in Fredericksburg, Virginia. Russell worked at the Pentagon and gave us a VIP tour there. He had a good friend who had special clearance to the White House and Capitol. At the White House we got to go to rooms that are off limits to the general public, including the Oval Office and the Newsroom.

The Newsroom was full of reporters and we got to go up front. One of the reporters asked the name of our town's newspaper. It was kind of ironic that my newspaper was the Liberal News, but not the fake news that usually comes out of that place.

After D.C. we drove to an Amish Community in Pennsylvania. The following day we were driving around looking over the country when Wilma suggested we stop at one of the Amish stores and check it out.

While we were in the store, my cousin Jerry Boles and his wife Annette came over to say "hi." Jerry lived in Coffeyville, Kansas at the time and we hadn't seen them in years! The odds of that happening must have been a million to one. They were on their way to vacation in Maine and Nova Scotia.

Now for the rest of the story....Wilma and Annette's relationship had been strained a little bit years earlier. It was the day we celebrated Barney & Grandma's 50th wedding anniversary. All the Crockett, Boles, and Quackenbush families met at the Blue Top Restaurant for Sunday dinner and then we went back to their house in Irwin to visit.

The men were sitting out on the front porch as usual. Annette and her little girl, Felicia, were walking around in the front yard. Felicia, who was two at the time, was carrying her little doll. Keith was four. For some reason*, Keith ran up to her, grabbed the doll and threw it over the fence.

Felicia went to crying and Annette took after Keith. Keith was running for his life when Wilma heard the commotion. She started chasing Annette. You know you don't mess with a mama bear and her cub.

One of the uncles on the porch (probably Uncle Ray) said it was just like old times when Bob and Jerry would start fighting and Aunt Betty and Aunt Jean would wade into it to defend their own boy.

Keith thought his time bomb was one step away.

Felicia Boles, Keith Crockett, Brent Peters
Great-Grandparents Myrtle & Barney Crockett
at their home in Irwin, MO on their 50th wedding anniversary

*Editor's Note: Perhaps the "reason" was that often repeated phrase:
"The apple doesn't fall far from the tree."

Chapter 39
Red River Trips

One of our landlords, Jake Sweatt, told me about a cabin he had at Red River, New Mexico. He said it was a beautiful place in the mountains and we should go sometime. We never got invited to stay in the cabin but there were a lot of places to camp.

We had a ten-foot pickup camper. It was supposed to sleep six but that never worked out very well. The table made into a bed and three could sleep in the bed over the cab. We added a cot in the aisle.

One summer Dean and Sandra Buffington went with us. The camp that we stayed at was next to the river. Denny and Louise had borrowed Grandpa Bunton's pickup and camper so they and their boys, Kevin and Scott, were camping beside us.

One day Kevin was squirting Dean with a water gun. Dean said, "Kevin, if you squirt me one more time, I'll throw you in the river."

Well, Kevin shot him and true to his word, Dean threw him in the river. Once again, a mama bear got really upset.

The next summer when we went back, Doug Carpenter went with us. Doug had worked for us that summer and when we got done haying, we took off. The town of Red River had a place where the kids could hang out. Keith and Doug went there, probably hoping to meet some girls.

Keith started playing air hockey with several different kids. When a Mexican boy saw that he was winning every time, he asked Keith to play against him. Keith beat him.

"Play again," the boy said. Keith beat him again and again, and each time the boy would get a little madder.

I asked Keith, "Did you let him win so he would leave you alone?"

"NO! I wasn't about to let him win!"

Later on when we were visiting with the Legans, we told them about our trips to Red River. They said that the next time we planned to go, they would like to go with us.

It was 1980 and we were having one of the worst droughts ever. I said, "Everything here is burnt up. Why don't we go to the mountains?" We called up Legans and they said they could get away too, so we chose a date to leave. Ken said they had a Jeep he would tow. I told him I was going to take two motorcycles so we would have plenty of toys.

This trip, it was Wilma, Michelle, and me along with Phil Charlton and Wilma's mother, Rosie, all piled in the pickup and camper. I think I had to fill up with gas every 150 miles. I got about five miles per gallon. I was hauling my 750 Honda and Michelle's 125.

One afternoon, Phil and I decided to take the bikes and go for a ride. We started going on a good gravel road but it didn't stay good very long. It was getting steeper and in worse condition. We decided that maybe we had better go back. We came to a road that went down a steep grade. When we got to the bottom...OOPS! A sign said "Private Property. Do not enter."

Now the 750 is not a dirt bike and it wouldn't climb back up that hill. We had no choice but to go on. Luckily, we found another road and made it back to town without getting shot or arrested.

The next day Ken said that someone told him about a lake way up in the mountains. It would be very steep, but his Jeep could make it fine. Ken and I decided to try to get up there. It was so steep that you could not turn up one switchback without backing up to get up the next one. About halfway up something broke in his gear shift. We were stuck in reverse. How in the world were we going to get down around the switchbacks when all we had was reverse?? We made the first one, so we kept on going. We backed all the way into town and didn't use the Jeep anymore.

The next day I decided to take the 750 and stay on the highway for a mountain ride. I rode down to Questa where there is the Rio Grande Gorge National Recreation Park. It had been a beautiful day but up popped an afternoon. storm. It started hailing so I found a restroom and got out of the hail. Seemed like it took forever for it to pass, but when it did, I started back to Red River.

On the way, a bumble bee hit me on the side of my face and blew back into my ear inside my helmet. I was able to stop, get my helmet off, and get him out without being stung. Lucky bee.

Ken had broken the hitch on his Jeep. He found a welding shop to get it fixed. When he was there, he met a cowboy and found out he was single. Ken told him that he knew a lady he should take on a date. The cowboy asked Rosie out and with our encouragement she went out with him. That was the only time she had ever gone out with anyone since she'd lost Harold. The cowboy wrote her a couple of letters but she never responded.

Chad Fast & Tom

Chapter 40

Last Summer Trip to Red River

In 1982, Michelle was going with a boy from Lockwood named Preston Eagles. We were talking about going to Red River. Preston said his sister had a fifteen-foot pull trailer that we could borrow and have room for everyone. With all that space with our camper and that trailer, Keith said they would go too. Dana was just two months old at the time. Keith borrowed Bruce Barker's dune buggy and pulled it out there with his Monte Carlo.

Uncle Everett and Cousin Sandy and Gary Todd also had their buggies out there so we had plenty of toys to play with. All was going great until one night a big rainstorm came up. Heavy rain. I was hoping the river wouldn't come up and wash us away. I stepped out of the trailer and I went knee-deep in mud. Everything we had outside was covered in mud. The city had been building a lagoon just above us and the dam had washed out with all that rain. Our luck: we were in the only campsite that was affected.

The next day we had to dig what we could find out of the mud, then go to a car wash and wash the camper and trailer the best we could. It took all morning. Nothing we could do after that but head home.

What a way to top off our camping trips there. That was our last summer at Red River.

Chapter 41

Lake City, Colorado

One day, John Rawlings called and said he and Judy had a place rented at Lake City, Colorado. He was going to take his Jeep and we should come with them. I threw on the camper, put two motorcycles on a trailer and off we went. This time, Doug and Michelle were the ones going with us. We found a campground a couple of miles west of Lake City.

The next day we went east of town where an old road went up the mountain to an old ghost town. The town had been an old mining camp. All the buildings were still standing and in pretty good shape. After exploring the town, we noticed the road went on up. Doug and I were on motorcycles. John had all the girls in his Jeep. We got to the top of the mountain and saw that the road went over the Continental Divide. We agreed we should go down the other side. The road was a lot steeper going down. Sometimes Doug and I would have to lay the cycles down and slide a little way. When we got down, we ran into a fence with a gate that was locked. No way could Doug and I go back up so we went down along the fence and found a place we could get out. To circle around on the highway to Lake City would be quite a long way. We didn't know if we would have enough gas to make it but we did.

John said there was a place where we could rent a Jeep and go over Engineer Pass to Silverton. We got the Jeep and headed out. The road was very rough, narrow and steep. One place was VERY steep and John had stopped at the top. I didn't know that there was room to pull beside him so I told the kids that when I stopped, they should jump out and put some rocks behind the tires. They did and we were all shaking by this time. What John could see, we couldn't.

We bounced on into Silverton, ate lunch then drove to Ouray and took a different pass back to Lake City. After getting back safely, we decided it had been worth it.

John Rawlings & Tom
Life-long Friends

Chapter 42

Fishing Trips

In 1986, Pioneer was having a dealer meeting in Des Moines, Iowa. Roy Clark was going to have a show for us. I told Wilma we could go up to Wisconsin and visit Larry Bunton for a couple of days, then come back through Des Moines.

I told Grandpa Bunton about our plan. He said he would like to go so Larry's girls could get to know their Great-Grandpa. He was 90 years old at that time. I told him about going to see Roy Clark but that didn't interest him at all. Grandpa always thought singing was just pure noise.

Larry had a favorite lake nearby and wanted to take Grandpa fishing one last time. We grabbed a bucket of leaches and drifted all afternoon. Didn't catch a thing.

Larry said the next day we should go up to a lake about a hundred miles north. Same thing: no fish. On the way home Larry stopped by the lake we'd been on the day before. His friend was just loading his boat on the trailer and showed us his cooler full of fish. Just our luck.

On the way home, I stopped at a rest stop so everyone could use the restroom. Apparently, Grandpa had loosened his belt during the drive. When he got out of the car, his pants fell to the ground. What a frightful sight. Wilma was more embarrassed than Grandpa.

And yeah, he didn't go to see Roy.

In 2008 while Keith was shelling corn at Sweatt's he backed up and hit a tree with the back of the combine. It hit the straw chopper and ruined it. I found a place in Illinois that had used combine parts. I told Denny & Louise that we could go up to Larry's and fish a couple of days and pick up a straw chopper on the way home.

Larry and Yvonne lived in a place next to the Wisconsin River. I told Larry I would like to try fishing in Wisconsin again. He said that since it was the middle of September, everyone had already winterized their boats but we could fish off the shore of Lake Michigan. Yvonne's brother lived on the way and we could borrow some poles and lures from him.

We drove east of Green Bay where the Fox River empties into Lake Michigan. That time of year, salmon and trout were coming out of the lake into the river. Yvonne's brother was the first to catch a salmon, then Denny and Larry. I hadn't had a bite so I went out and fished on the lakeside. The guys were ready to go, but I wanted to try a little longer.

Finally, I caught a nice big salmon. My one fish in Wisconsin.

Chapter 43

Deep Sea Fishing

In 2016 we were looking for a place to go on vacation. Michelle suggested we go to Destin, Florida. I got on Priceline and found a place on the beach in Destin. The condo had two bedrooms so I asked John and Judy Rawlings if they would like to go with us and they said yes.

One evening we went down to the Marina to watch the fishing boats come in. We walked around and looked at what they'd caught that day. John and I decided to take a full day trip because those went out further in the Gulf and bigger fish were caught.

We were told that when we got a bite we should reel in fast or the fish would get in a hole or behind a rock and couldn't be pulled out. I caught a big red snapper but when I got it to the boat all I had left was a big head. A shark had used my fish for a meal. Along with John and me, there was a man and his son on the boat. Everyone was catching some nice fish.

I hooked into something big and the captain was yelling, "REEL!" I was trying! It was bigger than I could reel so the man from Georgia took my pole. When he got it close to the boat, we saw it was a six-foot bull shark. He wanted to take it in and hang it up at the Marina, but I think the first mate cut the line.

I don't think the captain wanted to pull a shark thirty miles back to the dock. He probably didn't have a gun to shoot it either.

Chapter 44

Worst Vacations Ever

Ranking #1:

Pioneer had a multiple state convention in St. Louis. George Born rented a bus to take everyone from his district. At the convention they had a drawing for different prizes. We were the lucky winners of two tickets to a St. Louis Cardinal baseball game and two nights at the Adams Mark Hotel.

I suggested to Doug and Michelle that we make a trip out of it. We could go to Six Flags one day, then the next day go to the zoo and the ball game that night.

"Yes, that sounds like the kids would love that," Doug said. "Why don't we take my folks' van? We would have a lot more room." That sounded good so that was what we did.

At Six Flags, Kiley was too short for most of the rides so she wasn't in a very good mood for most of the day. Doug said, "Why don't you let me win some stuffed animals for you?" He was lucky and won a couple of big ones, so things were better.

We stayed the night in the town of Pacific. Cousin Marilyn lived close by so the next morning we drove to her place. Her husband Buck had passed away and she was getting ready to have a sale. In their shop, Marilyn had a big fan running. This fan was about three feet tall. For some reason, Kiley put her hand in it. Luckily, she was on the backside so she wasn't hurt badly. We didn't stay too long and went on to St. Louis.

This was in August and it was pretty warm. Just after we left Marilyn's, the air conditioner quit on the van. Roll down the windows; we'll make do.

We went to the zoo but it was so hot we didn't stay very long. We got to the hotel and found out that the van was too tall to go into the hotel parking lot. They told us we would have to use public parking which was about two blocks from the hotel. We unloaded all our luggage and the sun tea jar out in front of the hotel. Doug and I finally found a place to park. It didn't look very safe but what else could we do?

While the girls and Chad were waiting for us to get back, Chad was telling a high-class lady how his ol' grandpa had won them their tickets to the Cardinals game. Michelle didn't think the lady was too impressed.

The ballfield was only a couple of blocks from the hotel so the girls said that while Doug, Chad and I were at the game, they would go shop in the stores near the hotel. It was getting close to six in the evening when a cop asked what they were doing.

"Just shopping," they told him. He said that all the stores closed at 6:00 and it wasn't safe for them to be out in that area.

Shopping was over so they decided to go back to the hotel to go swimming. They were putting on their bathing suits when Kiley disappeared. In a panic, they found her in the hallway without any clothes on. She had seen how the card would unlock the door and she thought she would try. Their night wasn't going too well, so they decided to just stay in the room until the ballgame was over.

I had called Cousin Kenny Reaves and told him that we were going to the game. He said he would go with us. Afterwards, Kenny went back to the hotel with us. He said people would be shooting each other just two blocks north. We were glad they would be two blocks north.

Oh, that's where we parked the van! Sure enough, the van was broken into. About all that was in it was Kiley's stuffed animals so that's what was taken. To get in, they'd broken off the door handle. So, there we were with no air conditioning and a door that wouldn't shut. Let's go home!!

We were a few miles down I-44 when all traffic came to a stop. No A/C and we were cooking. It took forever before we finally got moving again. We went on down the road another 100 miles and it happened again. And it took forever again. We saw a road going north that would be a lot out of the way, but it was better than sitting still. A six-hour trip from St. Louis took ten hours but we finally got home. Boy, that was fun!

#2 on the list:

A "few years earlier" with Cousin Larry
Tom Crockett, Jessie & Emmet Bunton and Larry Bunton

In the Summer of 1974, we put the camper on our pickup and went to Wausau, Wisconsin to visit Cousin Larry Bunton and his wife, Marlene. The day after we got there, Larry had to go to work. Since they lived on the edge of town, Larry told us there were a lot of trails nearby and Keith and I could take his dirt bike and play around.

One of the trails went up a real steep hill. I told Keith, "I think I can make it to the top."

"Better not try," he said, "it's too steep and you will never make it."

Well of course, I had to show Keith that I was good enough to make it to the top. I got a big run at it and almost made it! What I hadn't seen from the bottom was a big tree root that went across the trail. So, I crashed and burned but I wasn't hurt and didn't hurt the bike.

"I told you so," Keith said.

Okay, we'll just pretend that never happened.

The next day Larry said, "Why don't we go up to Lake Tomahawk and go camping?" That sounded good. He said we could rent some canoes and go fishing.

We rented two canoes. Larry and Keith went in one; Wilma and I in the other. We paddled over by Larry and Keith and saw Keith's cork going all over. We told them, "Good luck!" and kept on going.

Larry said that Keith had hooked a big muskie but it broke the line before they could get it in the canoe. Larry had fished in Wisconsin most of his life and had never caught a muskie. Keith hooked one on his first try with a cork and worm.

The next morning we said goodbye to Larry and Marlene and headed north to Lake Superior and then on north to Canada. We were getting close to International Falls, Minnesota, when we heard a crash. Keith and Michelle were riding in the back of the camper. They were throwing a ball back and forth when Keith threw it through the window on top of the bed. We found a lumber yard and bought glass to fix it.

Back on the road we crossed the border into Canada and camped at Lake of the Woods. The next morning we were driving around the lake when we heard another crash. Keith had tried to get us to stop because he needed to go to the bathroom. We didn't hear him, so he kicked at the window, and it broke.

He had a pretty bad cut so we needed to get to a hospital. Winnipeg was the closest big town so that was where we went. We didn't know where to go so we stopped and asked a guy on the street where we'd find the nearest hospital.

When we got there, I grabbed Keith and carried him. We met some Nuns and one of them asked what I was doing.

I said, "My son cut his foot and needs stitches."

She said, "This is not that kind of hospital."

So we searched again and finally got to a hospital and Keith got his stitches. He still hadn't gotten to pee.

By that time, I decided it was time to head south and go home.

And #3: Sometimes it's just feelings that get hurt.......

For Christmas break in 1974 we decided to take the kids to Disney World in Florida. Wilma suggested we ask her folks to come with us. They thought it sounded fun and yes, they'd like to go.

We loaded up our eight foot camper and the six of us plus Michelle's dog, Roscoe were off to Florida. After our day at Disney World, Harold said that he'd always wanted to go to Key West.

Why not? Let's go. We spent the night at Key Largo and from there drove on to Key West. That is a distance of 133 miles of mostly bridges and just a few islands. After we arrived, we looked over the town of Key West and saw there wasn't much to do there so we started back.

The first oil shortage had hit and you were only allowed to put so much gas in your tank at a time. The '74 Chevy pickup hauling a camper loaded with six people and a dog didn't get very good gas mileage. We would put in our ten gallons and then get in line again for another ten. We were going to be going across Alligator Alley from the east side of Florida to the west at night. There would be nothing but Everglades so running out of gas would not be good. Another shocking thing was that gas had gone up to fifty cents a gallon.

We made it across the Everglades and spent the night at Fort Myers Beach. Wilma's mom, Rosie had read you could go to Sanibel Island and find gorgeous seashells along the beach.

We heard there was a big ice storm heading south. I thought we'd better head home and not get caught in the ice. You had to pay quite a bit to get across to the Island and it would kill another day. I made the decision we would head home.

When I said hurt feelings, Rosie didn't speak to me the rest of the way home.

Chapter 45

Red Eye Special

Spring Break, 1991, John Rawlings invited us to go snow skiing at Red River, New Mexico with his wife Judy, daughter Jenelle and her friend, Jackie Short. Wilma and I loaded up in John's van.

We left around 5 p.m. and drove all night in the rain. We talked about how welcome that rain would be for the new pond John had just built at Keith's. It never rained at home though.

We arrived at Red River mid-morning. The first thing to do was to rent boots and skis. The girl asked me what size boots I wore. I told her 10 ½ Triple E. Then she asked, "What color do you want?" Not really. The choice I had was either too narrow or too long. I guessed maybe the best would be to take the 11 ½.

The next question was what size skis I wanted: long or short? I again didn't have a clue. "Long, I guess." Right off the start I made two wrong choices.

We went up to the bunny slope for rookies. John had been skiing a couple of times, so he started giving me advice. "Snap on one ski, then the other."

If you use the formula to figure the speed of gravity at 15 feet per second squared, it took one third of a second before I hit the ground. I'm zero for three so far.

Now we needed to get on the lift and go to the top of this little hill. Getting on was okay but to get off you ski down a little slope and turn downhill. Zero for four. I crashed and burned and now I'm in the way of little kids trying to miss me. I got up and fell ten times before the bottom of the little bunny slope.

So far this is a lot of fun.

John said, "Why don't we go up on top of the mountain where there won't be as many little kids. You can practice up there."

Okay, we go to the top and there were no kids, but the safe way down was the hall road to the café on top. It had been used that day so it was full of jeep tracks. There was a black guy that was just as good as I was. We had a race to see which one of us could crash the most.

I told John that if I could have caught him going down, I would have broken a ski over his head. Boy, that hot tub sure felt good that night. It was the most fun I'd had all day.

The next day went a little better. I could sometimes ski all the way down the bunny slope without falling.

Chapter 46
Second Red Eye Special

In 1994, John said we could catch a bus in Kansas City, Kansas to go skiing in Colorado. We could rent all of our gear in KC and have it when we got to Dillon, CO. The bus would have a few places to lie down and we might even get a little sleep.

Brent Fast had worked for me that summer so I asked him and Chad if they wanted to go. Both said yes, so we drove to Kansas City, got on the bus and rode all night.

An old friend from Liberal, Larry Terrell and his neighbor were also on the bus. Larry said they went on this trip three or four times a year so they could tell us what to do.

The first day we were to ski at Breckinridge and on the second we'd be at Copper Mountain. I told the boys I would pay for them to go to ski school and learn how to do it the right way. The two of them weren't the same age so they were in separate classes.

Chad was a mess in his class. He didn't know left from right and was always going the wrong way. After they finished, they told me that had been a waste of their time and my money.

Larry said, "I'll teach them boys how to ski."

I told him, "Have at it. Good luck!"

I think I had altitude sickness or maybe it was fear of the slope. I didn't try to ski that day. That night Larry told me the boys did great and could really ski well.

The next day I felt much better. I thought to myself, "I'll try Copper." I picked out the easiest slope I could find. I was by myself because the rest of the guys wanted something more challenging.

That night on the bus ride home, one of the girls said, "Did you see that guy run over the 'Slow' sign? They all laughed.

Yeah, that was me. But if you missed it, it will be on "Not the Top Ten" on ESPN in the morning.

That was it for me. No more snow skiing.

Chapter 47

A Health Problem or
Three of My Own

The first of July 2016, I knew something wasn't quite right. I didn't feel bad, but I didn't feel good either. We had Paul Choning redoing our fishpond. He needed some large rocks to build the waterfall. I told him I had some large rocks up at my pasture at Bronaugh. Keith and I went up and got a load with the tractor and loader, so we had some large ones.

When I got back home with the tractor I parked and started to the house. When I got to the deck that was as far as I could go. I sat down.

When Chad saw me, he asked, "Are you all right?"

I said, "I think I have a high fever."

When he checked it, he said, "You better go to the ER."

After we got to Pittsburg, they started testing everything. The nurse said, "You're very sick so you need to stay overnight until we can figure out what the problem is."

I told them that some neighbors had tick fever so maybe that was what I had. They began treating me for that.

The next morning, they did an echocardiogram on my heart and thought that I had too much fluid around it. With that problem I needed to go to Freeman Hospital in Joplin.

At Freeman's they were still treating me for tick fever with higher and higher strength antibiotics. Test after test and I didn't get any better. They thought maybe it was my gall bladder but I'd need more tests.

They asked if I'd ever taken Penicillin. "Yes," I answered, "when I was a kid, I think I did."

They started giving me Penicillin in the vein. About an hour later, I started freezing and I couldn't breathe. I couldn't stop shaking. I looked

over and my family members were down on their knees praying. I thought my time bomb was about to go off. The nurse kept saying, "Relax! Relax!"

How do you relax when you can't breathe? After what seemed like forever, I started catching my breath. I'd had an allergic reaction to the Penicillin they were giving me.

Keith heard the Dr. say, "The old man should have known he was allergic to Penicillin." He called me an old man. I don't know why.

Off to ICU and more tests. Keith asked the Dr., "Why don't you take out his gall bladder?"

The Dr. answered, "Do you want me to kill him?" Up to this point they had been trying real hard to do just that.

After twelve days of hell, they took out my gall bladder one night and I went home the next day.

The next time I was in Freeman Hospital was to have shoulder replacement surgery. Dr. Twess did the surgery and said it went great. After falling off Cyclone, getting run over by Bainter skiing and trying to pound steel fence posts into frozen ground, my shoulder was worn out. When it got too painful to cast a rod and reel, it was time for replacement.

In July 2019 we went with Michelle and family to Navar Beach, Florida. Chad and Sarah were getting married on the beach. I noticed that walking on the sand caused me to get out of breath. I would stop for a couple of seconds and everything would be okay again. Then I started having heartburn, but a Tums would take care of that. Those were a couple of warning signs that I missed.

That fall I had neck pain, so I went to a Chiropractor. After he worked on my neck I stopped running out of breath. I thought that whatever was wrong had been fixed.

A couple of months later, the shortness of breath came back. I thought it must be because I was 79 years old.

Things started getting worse, so I went to Carla Reed, our Nurse Practitioner in Liberal. After listening to my heart, she said I should see a heart doctor. I told her that I had an appointment with a heart doctor in Joplin, but it was over a month away. She told me that if I had any pain in my chest I should go to the ER.

The day after Christmas, Michelle said, "I'm taking you to the ER at Mercy in Joplin." I didn't argue with her.

After the exam they said there was a serious problem with my heart. I was admitted to the hospital. The next morning the heart doctor on staff was Dr. Ko. He ordered a stress test and echocardiogram. After he got the results, he said that if I didn't do anything I wouldn't last a year.

Dr. Ko said he wanted to do a heart catheterization, but we should wait until after the holidays. They had a problem setting a date but finally got one. Just before I was to go, Wilma tested positive for Covid 19 so I had to wait two more weeks.

I finally had the test. Dr. Ko looked around the screen and asked, "You still awake?"

"Yes."

"You shouldn't be here. You are a miracle. You're over 90% plugged on the left and 100% plugged on the right side." He said that heart bypass was the best option.

He had a heart surgeon come in and talk to me. He said he was leaving town for a few days so he would turn it over to another surgeon. The next morning Dr. Brown came in and said that since I was on Eliquis, we should wait five more days before surgery. He also said there was a 20% chance I wouldn't wake up.

I said I would go home and come back when it was time for the surgery.

That's when he said, "You are a *ticking time bomb*. You'd never make it back to Joplin."

That's where the expression ticking time bomb came from.

The next morning Dr. Ko came in and said he didn't like the odds that Dr. Brown had for me. He said he could get three stents, maybe four in my heart and I would be good for ten to fifteen years.

I told him I thought that would do me just fine.

The next afternoon, Dr. Ko got the three stents in and I got to go home the day after that. He set me up to do physical therapy at Lamar Hospital. Of course, I didn't think I needed therapy. Chellie Gardner, the heart nurse at the Clinic called and wanted me to come to Lamar to talk to her. She finally convinced me to give it a try.

She said she opened the Clinic at 6 a.m. so I could come anytime. I told her that it wouldn't be at 6 but I would try 8. I went a couple times at 8 but it was very crowded, so I started going at 6 a.m. I got done with my therapy in June, but I still go to Lamar and exercise three days a week.

Chapter 48
Living by Faith

God has always been with me, and I wouldn't be here without Him. We are all ticking time bombs. We don't know the day it will go off, but it will go off for each one of us. God has our days numbered so we need to be ready.

I have been blessed with:

The perfect wife: Wilma

Two wonderful kids: Keith and Michelle

Five* super grandkids: Dana, Ashley & Bret Crockett, Chad & Kiley Fast (*) Keith and Melanie lost a boy before he was born but we will get to see him one day.

Eight precious great-grandkids: Clay, Hadlee, Sadie, Addie, & Cash Meadows, Owen & Riley Myers, Landry Marti, and Cooper Fast.

Five Generations
Tom Crockett, Marjorie Bunton Crockett Jones,
Emmet Bunton, Dana Crockett, Keith Crockett

Five Generations
Tom Crockett, Keith Crockett, Clayton Meadows,
Dana Crockett Meadows, Marjorie Bunton Crockett Jones

Five Generations
Tom Crockett, Marjorie Bunton Crockett Jones, Landry Marti,
Michelle Crockett Fast, Kiley Fast Marti

John 14:1-3

"Don't let your hearts be troubled. Trust in God, and trust also in Me. There is more than enough room in my Father's home. If this were not so, I would have told you. I am going to prepare a place for you. When everything is ready, I will come and get you, so that you will always be with Me where I am."

John 14:6

Jesus told them, "I am the way, the truth, and the life. No one can come to the Father except through Me."

When our great-grandson Clay passed away from a sudden illness at only fourteen months old, Gayla Charlton and Ruth Gazaway gave Wilma a <u>Women of Faith Study Bible</u>. I was looking through it when I came across this reading. It wasn't an accident that I opened it up to this:

"There is no such thing as premature death. Job 14:5 states, 'Man's days are determined; You have decreed the number of his months and have set limits he cannot exceed.'

"And **Psalm 139:16** says, 'All the days were written in your book before one of them came to be.'

"I find that realization comforting. In fact, it could be a cheer-up thought. To recognize God's sovereign determining of the number of days each of us is to have on earth relieves me of nagging questions like, 'If I had just done this, eaten that, not eaten that, stayed home, not stayed home...'

"This is not some kind of Christian fatalism in which we assume it doesn't matter if we take health and safety precautions. On the contrary, Scripture says our bodies are the temples of the Holy Spirit, and we must respect them as well as do our part in preserving them. But tension is released in me as I remember that the number of my days is in His hands and not mine.

"Based on Scripture, we do not die prematurely. We are ushered into God's presence at the time He has chosen for us."

--Marilyn Meberg

Epilogue

The grandkids thought it would be neat if I would read them the book I'd written. We got together on Wednesday, March 15th, 2023. This was the first time all the family had been together here in a long time. We planned to start at 6 p.m. I went to Chicken Mary's and picked up dinner and was back by 6.

We had just prayed when someone knocked on our front door. The man said, "I am Jerald Swarns, your new neighbor. I think you might have a heifer having trouble calving."

I told him my grandson had seen her but thought she had about had it. I thanked him and said that I would go out and check on her. Doug said he would go with me. We got in the pickup and drove down to where she was. After watching for a while, we decided she wasn't going to have it by herself.

"Let's get the Ranger and drive her up to the corral." Then I told Doug there was a big mud hole just before we could get to the corral and that might be a problem.

Well, I was right. She would turn every time we got her close to the mud. Doug got out of the Ranger to head her off and went in up to his knees in the muck and couldn't move. He finally got out and after four or five more attempts to get her past the mud hole, I said, "We need more help!" About that time, Keith and Chad came out.

I said, "You both go get your Rangers and maybe with all three we can get her." While they were gone, I tried one more time. I got her close, but she turned and went back through the mud. This time coming back through the mudhole, I got stuck. I had a chain so as soon as Chad got back, he pulled me out.

Two Rangers weren't going to get the job done so we had to wait for Keith. Finally, with three we boxed her in and just hoped we could get through the mud! If any of us got stuck, it was all over but believe it or not, we got her in the corral at last.

In the mayhem, I had lost the calf pullers. Sure enough, they were in the mud hole. It wasn't easy, but we finally retrieved them. Now we had to get her in the head gate. Chad couldn't get it to open because the bull had scratched his back on it and broke the latch. At last, he got it open and we had the heifer caught.

Keith got the chain on the calf and was able to pull him out. He was still alive after all that mom had been through. Mom went right over and claimed her new son. All had turned out fine.

By this time, it was 8:00. We had to clean up and eat before anything else. The book reading got shortened to just a few chapters.

Everyone agreed this episode just had to be added to the tale of Time Bomb Tommy. So now you have it: one more exciting chapter of my life.

***

Wilma & Tom
with Grandad Barney Crockett's 1950 Chevrolet pickup truck

Grandma Crockett persuaded Barney on the way to Jasper to spend the extra $50
for the optional wrap around back windows in their new pickup.

Acknowledgements

I want to thank my editor, Kathy. If she hadn't taken on this job, this book wouldn't have happened. I told her that I considered spelling, periods, and commas optional.

She has taken the book from a D up to an A.

Love you,

Tom

Made in the USA
Monee, IL
08 January 2024

50391485R00090